THE IMAGE OF THE AGES

Bible Prophecy
Iraq/Babylon . . . Armageddon

With a Foreword by David Breeze

Huntington House Publishers

Huntington House Publishers
P.O. Box 53788
Lafayette, LA 70505

ISBN 0-910311-38-2

Printed in United States

Contents

Dedication

To my beloved son Edward Webber. My son encouraged me to write this book. He daily brings joy and happiness to me.

I am also indebted to my good friends and associates Ed and Mary Belle Steele for advisory and editorial assistance.

Foreword

To have "A sense of History" and a knowledge of the prophetic Word is to possess two most excellent gifts. This is because history continues to unroll before us in what seems more rapid fashion than ever. History by itself however does not reveal its meanings. The meaning of history is only sensed by those who have given themselves to the understanding and then the mastery of the prophetic Word of the living God. The Bible instructs us as to the method of understanding history by saying "We have also a more sure word of prophecy; where unto ye do well that ye take heed, as unto a light that shineth in a dark place, until the day dawn, and the day star arise in your hearts . . ." (Peter 1 : 19).

It will be obvious to the reader that my friend, Dr. David Webber, has given himself to the mastery of that sure Word of prophecy and has transmitted to us that valuable knowledge in *The Image of the Ages*.

Through all of history, man in his unspiritual state has involved himself primarily in the consideration of the things which he can see with his eyes. Empiricism has been, for the most part, the primary method of mans pursuit of knowledge. Having decided what he thinks to be the facts about a rock, a tree, a mountain or even the starry heavens, man quickly moves from mere knowledge to worship. The object of his contemplation often becomes the object of his worship. Man, with frightening regularity, turns that rock or that tree which he contemplates into his god—he makes of it a "graven image."

By this act of disobedience to the clear teaching of the Word of God, man leaves the path by which he may pursue the knowledge of the true God and becomes a stunted pagan. By worshipping images of his own making, man in every nation and in every age has turned from life and embraced spiritual death. From the days of ancient Babylon to the modern spiritual and commercial Babylon of our time, the races of men have continued to turn from the true God to worship and serve the creature more than the Creator. Man has "changed the glory of the uncorruptible God into an image made like to corruptible man, and to birds, and to four-footed beasts, and creeping things" (Rom. 1:23). In all times and especially in our time, the predictable result has come to pass "wherefore God also gave them up to uncleanness through the lusts of their own hearts, to dishonor their own bodies between themselves" (Rom. 1:24).

So it is that when man turns from the incorruptible God to an image of anything else, especially corruptible man, he drops into a state of dishonor, despair and finally utter corruption. Who can doubt that that is the path being pursued in our modern world?

Along with me, each one of the readers of this most instructive and perceptive volume will pray that its timeless truths will lead many in another direction beside pursuing the image and the imagery of these days. We dare to hope that there will be brought to pass in the lives of Christians, and indeed the onlooking world, the proper course of thinking which is advocated by the Apostle Paul when he said, "While we look not at the things which are seen, but at the things which are not seen: for the things which are seen are temporal; but the things which are not seen are eternal" (11 Cor. 4:18).

But of course, this is not an easy task. Our world with its glowing, seductive and attractive "things" can easily beguile us away from our better senses into the many new

Foreword

forms of paganism that can come upon us by pursuing what one writer calls "the false gods of our time." Sensing this difficulty, the Apostle Paul earnestly admonishes every reader of his epistle to the Colossians, saying, "If ye then be risen with Christ, seek those things which are above, where Christ sitteth at the right hand of God. Set your affection on things above, not on things on the earth" (Col. 3:1-2). This valuable advice could save the sanity and even the lives of many. We must labor to wrench our affections, our attention, yes our worship from the things of time and deliberately set them with fixed purpose on "things that are above." The image of the earthly must be made to recede in our easily seduced minds in order that the image of the heavenly may become paramount. What indeed is "spirituality" but having a mind which is set on those things which are above?

We all will be greatly aided in this pursuit by a careful reading of *The Image of the Ages*. Out of this study, we shall once more purpose to concentrate on those things which are in fact ageless, which are eternal. Soon our "visible world," with all of its images, its seductions, its beguilements, will pass away. Then we will find ourselves living in that world which is eternal. May a touch of that eternal reality come upon us today.

DAVID BREEZE

INTRODUCTION

In studying the Bible, I came to the realization that there is a special significance and connection to the word *image, imagine,* and *imagination.* I began to better understand why God hates imagery, and why He said: "Thou shalt have no other gods before me. Thou shalt not make unto thee any graven image. . ." (Exod. 20:3,4).

Man was originally made in the likeness and image of God to fellowship with his divine creator (Gen. 1:26). But when the first man, Adam, transgressed God's law, he lost his godlike image. After that, Adam begat sons in his own image and likeness (Gen. 5:3).

You will discover in this book that the nature of spiritual warfare consist of rebel man trying to exalt his image rather than worshiping the pristine God and exalting His image. The sum and substance of Humanism and the devil's original lie is that man can become his own god.

The old serpent said to Eve in the garden of Eden, "Ye shall not surely die: For God doth know that in the day ye eat thereof, then your eyes shall be opened, and ye shall be as Gods, knowing good and evil" (Gen. 3:4,5).

We also study the significance of the great image, in the form of a metallic man, which God revealed in a vision to Nebuchadnezzar: to reveal the course of human history and Gentile empires.

I would also suggest that this humanistic image of man's conquest (Dan. 2:31-45) is the very same image that comes

9

alive in Revelation 13:14-17. In Daniel, the standing image is silent, because Daniel is a sealed book (Dan. 12:4). But in Revelation, this terrible Frankenstein image of the last days comes alive and dominates all languages, peoples, and nations for three and a half years—the time period of Antichrist domination.

Imagery goes hand in hand with idolatry in the Scriptures, including man's worship of the sun, moon, and stars. In fact, Paul's reference to the image in Romans 1:23 is simply describing our modern day zodiac and man's fascination with the horoscope. This is the way people worship the sun, moon, and stars today.

Finally, the word image is very big in todays modern world of electronic technology. The image of the television screen increasingly impacts the mass audiences of the media. The image on the multi-computer screens almost totally dominates the world of big business, mega-banks and international commerce.

The uppermost thought in the minds of national leaders today is their image. The same thing can be said of politicians as well as preachers.

In the words of a recent camera commercial, it's all in the image.

One

IMAGES OF BABYLON—ANCIENT AND MODERN

In Daniel chapter 5, the handwriting on the wall reveals the fall of ancient Babylon to the Medes and the Persians. However, prophetic passages in Isaiah chapters 13 and 14, Jeremiah chapters 50 and 51, Revelation chapters 17 and 18, and numerous other Scriptures, speak of an end-time Babylon (Iraq) that would arise in the last days, which God would judge like Sodom and Gomorrah:

> And Babylon, The Glory of Kingdoms, The Beauty of the Chaldees' excellency, shall be as when God overthrew Sodom and Gomorrah. And the wild beasts of the islands shall cry in their desolate houses, and dragons in their pleasant places: and her time is near to come, and her days shall not be prolonged. (Isa. 13:19,22)

This end-time Babylon would be from the old Chaldean kingdom and would be located in the Land of Shinar (Zech. 5:5-11). Notice also the judgment of Babylon as recorded in the book of Revelation:

> And after these things I saw another angel come down from Heaven, having great power: and the Earth was lightened with his glory. And he cried mightily with a strong voice, saying, Babylon the great is fallen, is

> fallen, and is become the habitation of devils,
> and the hold of every foul spirit and a cage
> of every unclean and hateful bird. And a
> mighty Angel took up a stone like a great
> millstone, and cast it into the sea, saying,
> thus with violence shall that great city
> Babylon be thrown down and shall be found
> no more at all. (Rev. 18:1,2,21)

In the middle seventies we began to see occasional news items about rebuilding old Babylon and even the possibility of reconstructing the tower of Babel. Reportedly, large grants of thirty million dollars were bestowed upon Iraq for the express purpose of rebuilding Nebuchadnezzer's Babylon. These grants were given to Iraq by the United Nations and O.P.E.C. and individuals on at least three occasions.

Then an exciting article appeared in the *Los Angeles Times* Jan. 16, 1987 describing a projected international music festival on or near the site of the golden image of Daniel chapter 3. "New writing on wall—can Babylon relive its glory days" was the title of the article.

> "In the same hour came forth fingers of a
> man's hand, and wrote . . . upon the plaster
> of the wall of the king's Palace . . . and this is
> the writing that was written . . . God hath
> numbered thy kingdom, and finished it . . .
> Thou art weighed in the balances, and art
> found wanting" (Daniel 5). There is still
> handwriting   on   the   wall   of
> Nebuchadnezzar's Palace. Not as Apocalyptic
> as the message that the Bible says Daniel
> translated for King Belshazzar, it simply
> proclaims to all who pass through the
> portals of these time-worn ruins that "Pete
> was here."

> Today, little remains of the grandeur that
> was ancient Babylon, the city of Hammurabi
> and Nebuchadnezzar, the site of the hanging

gardens and the Tower of Babel, and of
course, the place where the famous handwriting on the wall spoiled Belshazzar's
dinner party. Nowadays graffiti defaces
what is left of the walls . . .

In a way, a veritable Babel of languages
clutter the restored white-washed walls . . .
the present intrudes upon Babylon in other
ways too. At the entrance to the ruins, next
to a half-size model of the great Ishtar Gate,
stands a 30-foot-high portrait of Iraq's
President Saddam Hussein, shown there as
a modern-day Nebuchadnezzar protecting
Babylon from its past and present enemies,
the Persians of neighboring Iran.

At a time when Iraq is hard pressed to continue paying for the costs of its six-year-old
war with Iran, Hussein has ordered that no
expense be spared to restore Ancient
Babylon to its former glory in time for an
international music festival that is scheduled
to be held here in September. The restoration
project, begun in 1978 before the start of the
Iran-Iraq war, was undertaken to save the
remnants of the city . . . However, Babylon
has assumed additional importance for the
government since the war broke out in
September 1980. Keen on establishing a link
between its current conflict with the Persians
and the legendary battles of the past, the Iraq
government has speeded up the reconstruction in order to make Babylon a symbol of
national pride.

In the haste, however, some western critics
suggest that Babylon is not so much being
restored to its former glory as it is being
turned into a three-dimensional
propaganda statement . . . Iraqi officials
bridle at criticism like this and say that when

the reconstruction is finished, the new Babylon will look just like the old one . . . Munir Bashir, who plays the lute and the ud, has ambitious plans for the music festival to be held in the restored amphitheater and other made-over parts of the 2,000 year old ruins from September 22 to October 22. "We will have musicians from all over the world, from Europe, Asia, Africa, and Arabia. From America we will have a famous movie star—I cannot say which one yet—and we have asked for Madonna." He said, why Madonna? "Because the Iraqi young people love Madonna." Madonna lives here with the Iraqi people" he added, pointing to his heart. "I hope Madonna will know this fact and will come." "The Iraqi's want this to be a great festival, like Baalbek in the old days," one diplomat said, "But with the war on, a lot of people are going to be afraid to come."

Bashir dismisses these fears as unfounded, noting that Babylon, 55 miles south of Baghdad on the Euphrates river, is well away from any fighting and has never been bombed. "Babylon is completely safe, he said. Also, "This is not just an Iraqi festival: he added, warming to his favorite subject. "It is a festival for the whole world, because Babylon was the capital of civilization once and has given the world so much. People from all over want to come to Babylon."

Talent already signed up for the festival includes ballet troupes from the Soviet Union and France, opera from Italy, folk dancers from Greece, Turkey, Poland, and Yugoslavia, Flamenco artists from Spain and Bedouin dancers from Saudi Arabia. "The movie stars who are our guests will each recite the laws of Hammurabi in their own languages," Bashir said, "Everything will be like it was in ancient Babylon," he added. "People will be given Babylonian costumes to wear and newly minted Babylonian money to spend." Even the food to be served will be based on 2,000-year-old recipes, he said."

In bringing together musicians from around the world to perform here, Bashir is attempting to grant Babylon a pardon from the biblical sentence imposed upon it in the book of Revelation, when a "Mighty" angel cast a stone into the sea and said: "So shall Babylon the great city be thrown down with violence, and shall be found no more: and the sound of harpers and minstrels, of flute players and trumpeters, shall be heard in thee no more."

The international music festival was held in old Babylon Sept. 22–Oct. 22 1987, but on a much smaller scale than originally planned. The rebuilding of ancient Babylon continued, but at a slow pace due to the eight years plus war between Iraq and Iran (Babylon and Persia again fighting).

After the war, Iraq, a nation of just over 17 million people, ended up with a debt of 80 billion dollars: one hundred thousand casualties, but no great damage to their cities.

Today, Iraq has become an awesome military power with a million man army, over five thousand tanks and more than five hundred aircraft. In spite of the fact that the Iraqi people live in the fertile crescent where civilization began, over 75 percent of their food supply is imported. This fact has made them very vulnerable to the blockade of the Western powers and the United Nations.

Because of the unexpected invasion of Kuwait, August 2, 1990, the Persian Gulf Crisis has once again brought the world to the brink of an explosive war in the Middle East.

The Helsinki Summit is just one of several conferences triggered by the sudden bellicose move of Saddam Hussein.

Quoting *Time*, Sept. 17, 1990 under the heading "A New World":

> It was certainly nothing that Saddam Hussein intended, but his invasion of Kuwait bore its most significant fruit on Sunday. For the first time since World War II, the leaders of the U.S. and the Soviet Union met each other not as cold war adversaries or even as wary rivals to make their competition more manageable, but as partners cooperating against a common enemy: Saddam, Presidents George Bush and Mikhail Gorbachev arrived in Helsinki fully agreed on their objective: An unconditional Iraqi pullout.

> Day before yesterday, such super power cooperation against a nation that had long been an ally of the Kremlin's would have been inconceivable, but their new Quasi alliance is the most striking, though very far from the only example of a proposition that has gathered force over the past six weeks: Saddam's power grab and the U.S. led opposition to it have so shaken up global political and power calculations that the world will never be the same.

The Helsinki summit was surprising, since it was Russia who has primarily armed Iraq and supplied them with military advisers, of whom 153 reportedly still remain in Iraq.

Rev. John Barela, with whom I have labored in the ministry more than a decade, addresses the subject of the Iraq war in the Bible, in his magazine, Oct. 1990:

> The Book of Jeremiah provides us with a graphic description paralleling the events we see taking place right before our very

eyes on daily television newscasts, in newspapers and in news magazines. Jeremiah chapter 50 verse 1 gives us the prophecy against Babylon, "The word that the Lord spoke against Babylon and against the land of the Chaldeans by Jeremiah the prophet." *U.S. News and World Report* reported the amazing fact that, "near the site of Babylon, which Saddam is rebuilding as a tourist attraction, a billboard features the president's profile alongside a picture of Nebuchadnezzar."

Could Saddam be the modern day Nebuchadnezzar the scriptures so vividly describe? Evidently Saddam thinks he is—he has declared it.

Verses 9 and 41 of the 50th chapter illustrate to us the fact that holy men of God spoke as they were moved by the Holy Spirit. We read in verse 9, "For Lo, I will raise and cause to come up against Babylon an assembly of great nations from the north country." Perhaps referring to NATO, Canada and the United States, have indeed set themselves in array against her.

Verse 41 of the same chapter also mentions the nations. We read "Behold, a people shall come from the north (perhaps referring to the Soviet Union and or Iran) and the great nation, (perhaps referring to the United States) and many kings shall be raised up from the coasts of the Earth."

Some of the countries that have already committed themselves militarily and economically are: Great Britain, France, West Germany, Turkey, The Netherlands, Canada, Japan, Egypt, Syria, and other Arab nations. These are only some of the nations which have become involved in the present crisis. An interesting note is the fact that Israel is not mentioned in the Jeremiah scenario as being involved in the Iraq war, and they have not taken an active part against Iraq in the present crisis.

We do not know if the time is near when God would utterly destroy Babylon: and use the nations in judgment against her, so that this ancient land might never be inhabited again. But it is amazing how the world has moved in almost total unanimity against Iraq after the sudden invasion of Kuwait.

Quoting *Time*, Aug. 20, 1990 "Putting On The Squeeze":

> *Diplomatic*—the U.N. security council condemned Iraq's invasion and annexation of Kuquait. So did the Arab league. *Economic*--the U.N. imposed mandatory sanctions, forbidding all member states to conduct business with Iraq. The European community, the U.S., and Japan froze Kuwait assets. *Military*—the U.S. deployed ground forces and air units to protect Saudi Arabia. Britain sent two squadrons of combat planes. Members of the Arab league sent troops. The U.S., Britain, France, Canada, Australia, West Germany, The Netherlands and Belgium moved to position naval vessels to enforce a potential blockade. The Soviet Union dispatched two ships as a precaution.

The idols or images of Iraq today are the huge pictures of Saddam Hussein, often three and four stories high, frequently accompanied by an imagined likeness of Babylon's first supreme ruler—Nebuchadnezzar. Hussein likens himself to Nebuchadnezzar and perhaps secretly believes that he is the reincarnation of this fearful monarch.

In exercising absolute powers, he is more often

compared to Hitler than to a monarch, in his penchant for cruelty and killing.

Theologians, have in the past, puzzled over some verses in Isaiah chapter 21, which could have a modern message for today's Babylon—Iraq. "The burden of the desert of the sea. As whirlwinds in the south pass through: so it cometh from the desert, from a terrible land" (Isa. 21:1).

It has been suggested that the desert of the sea is the Persian Gulf, where the critical blockade is gathered: and Iraq is the terrible land. Since the operation against Iraq is called desert shield, I immediately noticed the words in verse five—"Anoint the Shield." Also of interest, the phrase in verse thirteen "The burden upon Arabia."

If Isaiah chapter 21 is a prophetic portent for the last days, then verse fifteen would indicate that war in the Middle East could soon become a bloody Holocaust. "For they fled from the swords, from the drawn sword, and from the bent bow, and from the grievousness of war" (Isa. 21:15).

Since Jeremiah chapter 50 reads like a newspaper headline, rather than a centuries old prophecy uttered by the mouth of Jeremiah, let's examine a few cryptic verses in Jeremiah 51:

> Thus saith the Lord, behold, I will raise up against Babylon, and against them that dwell in the midst of them that rise up against me, a destroying wind: and will send unto Babylon fanners, that shall fan her, and shall empty her land: *for in the day of trouble they shall be against her round about.* Against him that bendeth let the archer bend his bow, and against him that lifteth himself up in his brigandine: *and spare ye not her young men*: destroy ye utterly all her host. Thus the slain shall fall in the land of the Chaldeans, and they that are thrust through in her streets. For Israel hath not been forsaken, nor Judah of his God, of the Lord of hosts: though their land was filled with sin against the Holy one

of Israel. Flee out of the midst of Babylon,
and deliver every man his soul: be not cut off
in her iniquity: for this is the time of the
Lord's vengeance: He will render unto her a
recompence. (Jer. 51:1-6)

Although Israel has heretofore not become involved in
the Persian Gulf Crisis, If war breaks out, Israel will doubtless become God's battle axe to utterly destroy wicked
Babylon—Iraq (See Jer. 51:20).

That God has determined judgment against
Babylon—the beginning of Gentile empires, the foul source
of Babylonish mysteries of the occult—is evident
throughout this chapter:

Behold, I am against thee,O destroying
mountain, saith the Lord, which destroyest
all the Earth: and I will stretch out mine hand
upon thee and roll thee down from the rocks,
and will make thee a burnt mountain. And
they shall not take of thee a stone for a corner,
nor a stone for foundations: but thou shalt be
desolate for ever, saith the Lord. (Jer.
51:25,26)

Verse twenty-six reminds us that many bricks and
building blocks from Babylon were in recent times carried
off to Baghdad for purposes of building that city. And bricks
properly inscribed and identified from Babylon have been
found in the streets and buildings of Baghdad. God's word
declares that this will not happen again. "Go ye out of the
midst of her," God said of Babylon,

and deliver ye every man his soul from the
fierce anger of the Lord. And lest your heart
faint, and ye fear for the rumour that shall be
heard in the land: A rumour shall both come
one year, and after that in another year shall
come a rumour, and violence in the land,
ruler against ruler. Therefore, behold, the
days come, that I will do judgment upon the
grave images of Babylon: and her whole

> land shall be confounded, and all her slain
> shall fall in the midst of her. Then the Heaven
> and the Earth, and all that is therein, shall
> sing for Babylon: for the spoilers shall come
> unto her from the north saith the Lord. (Jer.
> 51:45-48)

In these climatic verses, we see God's admonition to go out of Babylon before the destruction comes: even as hundreds of thousands have fled out of Iraq and Kuwait. Verse forty-six is a possible indication that the crisis develops in 1990, but the war breaks out in 1991. This is not a timetable, only an observation!

Jeremiah 51:47 addresses the subject of graven images, so we know that as the images of ancient Babylon perished, the images of modern Babylon will also be destroyed. Whether verse forty-eight indicates Russia or simply a NATO alliance is not conclusive. What is definitive, is that the end-time Babylon with all of her images of idolatry will be destroyed utterly: and the cradle of man's beginning will never be inhabited again.

Two

THE TRAIL OF THE IMAGE

The Bible is all about imagery and idolatry. Since the pristine creation of man, "made in the likeness and image of God" (Gen. 1:26), the image factor has been prominent in history and prophecy. The battle of the images includes God and man with the devil's dark image in the background playing man against God. As we will note in this chapter, man's image comes into sharp focus in the metallic man of Nebuchadnezzar's dream (Dan. 2:31-35). The interplanetary battle of the images is not resolved until the battle of Armageddon and the return of the Lord Jesus Christ, "the express image" of God the Father.

> God, who at sundry times and in divers manners spake in time past unto the Fathers by the prophets, hath in these last days spoken unto us by His Son, whom He hath appointed heir of all things, by whom also He made the worlds; being the brightness of His glory, and the express image of His person, and upholding all things by the word of his power, when he had by Himself purged our sins, sat down on the right hand of the Majesty on high. (Heb. 1:1-3)

Ever since man was exiled from the Garden of Eden, he has been trying to perpetuate his own image. The great image of Daniel chapter 2 is a prophetic panorama of manmade kingdoms and empires. Notice that the image of Daniel chapter 2 is in the form of a man composed of different metals. Let us read Daniel's description of the great image:

> Thou, 0 King, sawest, and behold a great image. This great image, whose brightness was excellent, stood before thee: and the form thereof was terrible.

> This image's head was of fine gold, his breast and his arms of silver, his belly and his thighs of brass his legs of iron his feet part of iron and part of clay.

> Thou sawest till that a stone was cut out without hands, which smote the image upon his feet that were of iron and clay, and break them to pieces.

> Then was the iron, the clay, the brass, the silver, and the gold, broken to pieces together, and became like the chaff of the summer threshing floors: And the wind carried them away, that no place was found for them: And the stone that smote the image became a great mountain, and filled the whole earth. (Dan. 2:31-35)

This monumental prophecy reveals the course of history and the destiny of empires. This metallic image was shown to Nebuchadnezzar in a dream and the interpretation of the dream was revealed in a vision to Daniel.

Traditionally, the head of gold is thought to be Babylon, the first world empire of the Gentiles. The breast and arms of silver depict the dual kingdoms of the Medes and Persians. The belly and thighs of brass foretell the conquest of Alexander and the Grecian Empire. The fourth kingdom is the iron empire of Rome with the Western capitol in Rome and the Eastern leg (or capitol) in Constantinople (today called Istanbul). The feet, part of iron and part of clay, signify the revived Roman Empire composed of monarchies and democracies.

But God gave Daniel His interpretation:

> Thou, 0 king, art a king of kings: For the God of Heaven hath given thee a kingdom, power, and strength, and glory, And wheresoever the children of men dwell, the beasts of the field and the fowls of the heaven hath he given into thine hand, and hath made thee ruler over them all. Thou art this head of gold.

> And after thee shall arise another kingdom inferior to thee, and another third kingdom of brass, which shall bear rule over all the earth.

> And the fourth kingdom shall be strong as iron: for as much as iron breaketh in pieces and subdueth all things: and as iron that breaketh all these, shall it break in pieces and bruise.

> And whereas thou sawest the feet and toes, part of potter's clay, and part of iron, the kingdom shall be divided: but there shall be in it of the strength of the iron, for as much as thou sawest the iron mixed with miry clay.

> And as the toes of the feet were part of iron, and part of clay, so the kingdom shall be partly strong, and partly broken.

> And whereas thou sawest iron mixed with miry clay, they shall mingle themselves with the seed of men: but they shall not cleave one to another, even as iron is not mixed with clay.

> And in the days of these kings shall the God of Heaven set up a kingdom, which shall never be destroyed: And the kingdom shall

not be left to other people, but it shall break
in pieces and consume all these kingdoms,
and it shall stand forever.

For as much as thou sawest that the stone
was cut out of the mountain without hands,
and that it break in pieces the iron, the brass,
and clay, the silver, and the gold: the great
God hath made known to the king what shall
come to pass hereafter: and the dream is
certain, and the interpretation thereof sure.
(Dan. 2:37-45)

Concerning Babylon, Daniel plainly says to King
Nebuchadnezzar, "Thou art this head of gold." Notice also
in Daniel 3:1, "The King made a golden image," evidently
an attempt to perpetuate his kingdom and/or image. Daniel
indicates that the second and third kingdoms, although
world empires, would decidedly and descendingly be in-
ferior to the first kingdom. The fourth kingdom, we will
examine more specifically, because of the dichotomy of its
role both in history and in prophecy.

The Word of God concerning the future of nations
reveals that the Roman Empire was to be broken into pieces.
When ten of the pieces which broke off formed an alliance
at the end of the age, then the world would know that the
coming of the Messiah to establish His kingdom over the
earth was near.

Rome appeared as a world power in 242 B.C. with the
conquest of Sicily. Gradually, the iron hand of Rome was
extended westward to Spain, northward to Germany and
England, and eastward to Egypt and Syria. The Roman
army under General Pompeius took protective custody of
Jerusalem in 63 B.C. completing the replacement of Greece
as the dominant world empire. The dominion of Rome over
its conquered territories was as brittle and unyielding as
iron in every respect. Taxes, goods, slaves, and produce
flooded the markets of Rome from all over the known
world.

Citizens of Rome lived like kings while the rest of the

world lived like paupers. All roads led to Rome. By the inspiration of God, Daniel said, "And the fourth kingdom shall be strong as iron: for as much as iron breaketh in pieces and subdueth all things: and as iron that breaketh all these, shall it break in pieces and bruise."

In the chronological order of world empires, Rome, (the iron kingdom), broke into pieces with each piece becoming a nation. Rome has never ceased to exist; it simply broke into independent nations, all dictatorships today can trace their governmental structure back to Rome. The two legs of iron represented Rome. The empire was divided into two parts—the Western division with Rome as its capital and the Eastern division with Constantinople for the capital. The two legs stood side by side as one empire until the iron empire began to deteriorate in the year A.D. 476. The break occurred first in the right leg. The position of nations (according to the Bible) is as they face Jerusalem.

In A.D. 773, Charlemagne became emperor of the Holy Roman Empire. In the year, A.D. 963, Italy was overrun by Germany, a province that Rome had difficulty keeping under subjection. The Germans absorbed the Western division of Rome and moved the capitol to Berlin. The Germans then claimed the throne of the Roman Empire and they named their king, "Kaiser," which is German for "Caesar."

The Eastern division of Rome, especially the southern part, gradually succumbed to rising Arab nationalism as promoted by Mohammed from A.D. 570 to A. D. 632. On his first military campaign into Asia Minor, Mohammed brought three thousand Christian idols back to Mecca. The churches of Asia did not heed God's warning issued in Revelation chapters 2 and 3, and their "candle-sticks were removed." However, the capital of the Eastern division of Rome was not conquered until A.D. 1453 by Mohammed II.

The Russians conquered and annexed much of the northern half of the Eastern division of Rome, including Armenia. One historical source notes that the Russians even occupied Constantinople for a time, and they established St.

Petersburg as the capital of Eastern Rome. Eventually the capitol was transferred to Moscow where it remains today. The Russians named their ruler, the *Czar*, which is Russian for *Caesar*. The Bolshevik Revolution, which was taken over by the Communists, replaced the government of the Russian Caesars by a system of commissars, or communist caesars. The board of communist caesars in Russia is presided over by a high caesar. The present chairman of the board is Gorbachev.

The relationship of the so-called "Free World" with communism has gone through a series of changes from allies, to direct confrontation, to peaceful coexistence and detente. The liberal propaganda has been that communism would mellow and change to a more yielding socialistic form of political ideology. But Russia is one of the iron pieces in the leg of the Gentile image, and iron cannot change its shape except it be melted down and recast. The very symbols of communism are iron: the iron hammer, iron sickle, and iron fist.

Daniel prophesied almost twenty-five hundred years ago that the Roman Empire would "break in pieces and bruise," and the prophet said the bruising would occur when anyone attempted to put the pieces together again. There have indeed been many such attempts, and as prophesied in the Bible, constant wars and bloodshed have resulted. The two greatest wars the world has ever known, World War I and World War II, began between nations of the old Roman Empire when someone attempted to put the image back together. But before World War I, numerous attempts were made, and one of the most notable of these was made by Napoleon.

Napoleon conquered all the western leg of Rome with the exception of England, and the emperor overran all the eastern leg of Rome with the exception of Moscow. He did occupy Moscow for a time, but he was not able to hold it. It was in Russia that he suffered a humiliating defeat from which his dreams for reuniting Rome never recovered. His vision was ultimately shattered at the Battle of Waterloo in

1815, and history records that Napoleon's final defeat was due to an act of God. It simply was not time on God's prophetic calendar for Rome to be revived as the kingdom of Antichrist.

After Napoleon, the next most serious attempt to weld together the pieces of iron was made by the Kaiser, or Caesar, of Germany in World War I. Then came World War II when Adolf Hitler of Germany and Benito Mussolini of Italy formed the Axis Alliance. Adolf Hitler made the same mistake that Napoleon made. He struck east at the old eastern leg of Rome while leaving England, an un-conquered portion of the western leg, and the United States at his rear.

After World War II, Russia, which still possessed the relocated capitol of Eastern Rome, was presented with a golden opportunity also to capture Berlin, which possessed the relocated capitol of Western Rome. But for over forty years Berlin has stood as the sole example of where the United States has constantly resisted Communist pressure. It is reported that after World War II, Eisenhower had to threaten to use the atomic bomb against Russia in order to obtain the partitioning of Berlin. In this dividing of the city, the old capitol buildings and sites remained in possession of the Allies instead of being given to Russia.

In spite of constant Communist pressure, including the Berlin blockade, the United States stood firm. It is not yet time for Rome to be reunited under one authority because that authority is reserved for Antichrist. With the reunification of Germany, however, we see a definite move in that direction.

But let us go back before the time of Rome and determine why man (originally made in the likeness and image of God) tries so hard to promote his own image, and why God hates imagery. In the beginning, God created man for Himself, to project His godly image in true worship and fellowship with God, and for man to have dominion over all the earth:

> And God said, Let us make man in our

image, after our likeness: And let them have dominion over the fish of the sea, and over the fowl of the air, and over the cattle, and over all the earth, and over every creeping thing that creepeth upon the earth.

So God created man in His own image, in the image of God created He him; male and female created He them.

And God blessed them, and God said unto them, be fruitful, and multiply, and replenish the earth, and subdue it: and have dominion over the fish of the sea, and over every living thing that moveth upon the earth. (Gen. 1:26-28)

But soon after man's sin and subsequent exile from the Garden of Eden, there was suddenly a great barrier between God and man, and man's profile subtly changed:

This is the book of the generations of Adam, In the day that God created man, in the likeness of God made He him: male and female created he them and blessed them, and called their name Adam, in the day when they were created.

And Adam lived an hundred and thirty years, and begat a son in his own likeness, after his image: and called his name Seth. (Gen. 5:1-3)

This noble creation erupted in concerted rebellion in the days of Noah which ended in the judgment of the great flood. Not many centuries later, man is again turning away from God and exalting his own image:

And the whole earth was of one language, and of one speech. And it came to pass, as they journeyed from the east, that they found a plain in the land of Shinar, and they dwelt there. And they said one to another, go to, let us make brick, and burn them

> thoroughly. And they had brick for stone, and slime had they for mortar. And they said, go to, let us build us a city and a tower, whose top may reach unto heaven: and let us make us a name, lest we be scattered abroad upon the face of the whole earth. And the Lord came down to see the city and the tower, which the children of men builded. And the Lord said, behold, the people is one, and they have all one language, and this they begin to do: and now nothing will be restrained from them, which they have imagined to do. (Gen. 11:1-6)

Please notice the word's *imagined* or *imagination* derived from the word *image*. Man, made in the likeness and image of God though in a darkened condition spiritually and morally, can eventually do whatever he can imagine; for example, go to the moon, split the atom, create human-like computers, i.e., robots.

Paul gives us a very enlightening commentary on the antediluvian society:

> For the wrath of God is revealed from Heaven against all ungodliness and unrighteousness of men, who hold the truth in unrighteousness because that which may be known of God is manifest in them, for God hath shewed it unto them.

> For the invisible things of him from the creation of the world are clearly seen, being understood by the things that are made, even his eternal power and Godhead: so that they are without excuse: because that, when they knew God, they glorified Him not as God, neither were thankful: but became vain in their imaginations, and their foolish heart was darkened.

> Professing themselves to be wise, they
> became fools, and changed the glory of the
> uncorruptible God into an image made like
> to corruptible man, and to birds, and
> four-footed beasts, and creeping things.
>
> Wherefore God also gave them up to
> uncleanness through the lusts of their own
> hearts, to dishonor their own bodies be-
> tween themselves: who changed the truth of
> God into a lie, and worshiped and served the
> creature more than the Creator, who is
> blessed for ever. Amen. (Rom. 1:18-25)

The interesting word *image* in verse twenty-three is a direct reference to the zodiac, created by man as a perversion of God's creation of the circular heavens (God's Bible in the stars) perpetuating man's image. The result is the daily horoscope by which many people order their lives. By virtue of almost unbelievable technology, man is almost ready to build his own God.

Nebuchadnezzar's standing, albeit silent, image (in the form of a man) suddenly comes alive in the book of Revelation:

> And He had power to give life unto the
> image of the beast, that the image of the beast
> should both speak, and cause that as many
> as would not worship the image of the beast
> should be killed.
>
> And he causeth all, both small and great, rich
> and poor, free and bond, to receive a mark
> in their right hand or in their foreheads: And
> that no man might buy or sell, save he that
> had the mark, or the name of the beast, or the
> number of his name.
>
> Here is wisdom: let him that hath
> understanding count the number of the
> beast: for it is the number of a man: and his

number is six hundred threescore and six.
(Rev. 13:15-18)

Notice again Daniel's description of the image of the ages. "Thou, 0 king sawest, and behold a great image. This great image, whose brightness was excellent, stood before thee; and the form thereof was terrible" (Dan. 2:31).

The great or gigantic standing image will be an imposing sight to the nations of the world. The brightness of the image could imply its worldwide appearance on satellite television and cable. The huge shining metallic image becomes an object of terror when it gains control of all the world and carries out the demonic orders of Satan's man: the Antichrist.

How will all this come about? Three examples will suffice to demonstrate the technology already in our grasp:

◆ Quoting from *The Magazine Proceeding of the Institute of Electrical and Electronics Engineers*, January, 1984:

> The Fifth Generation computer project aims at incorporating artificial intelligence into computing systems with logical inference capability used for natural language interpretations and the like. These new smart moves will be ready in the immediate future at just the time the market demand will explode. American and European competitors are now gearing up to meet this exciting new challenge.

> Do you realize what this all means? Within the next six years fifth generation computers will supersede our current most sophisticated supercomputers. Engineers have developed a robot that has camera eyes, temperature and radiation-measuring sensors, multi-jointed arms capable of complicated operations. Now, we already have robots which speak, obey spoken commands and identify shapes of objects, but they are mere prototypes of smart

robots. Robots are just one application, and robots are already making other robots! In less than six years, supercomputers will be one hundred times more powerful.

◆ The June 1984 edition of Popular Science states:

TV firms are readying receivers with computer chips that replace hundreds of components and process video in digital form. Computerized picture and sound circuits simplify TV alignment, noise and ghost reduction, teletext and videotex reception. They also make possible many totally new features, such as freeze-frame, color pictures within a picture zoom, 1,000-line images, automatic VCR programming and more.

Last fall, at the world's largest consumer electronics show in West Berlin, a Panasonic engineer gave me what looked like an ordinary TV infrared remote control. But when I used it, I learned that the matching 19-inch color receiver, to which I flicked commands was far from ordinary. The set, in a show demonstration room, had all the features of a current high-end model. Glowing in one corner of the main TV picture, though, was a separate five-inch TV image. One of the remote's many functions enabled me to instantly reverse these independent pictures; when I tapped a button, the small picture filled the screen, and the big image collapsed into a corner. But unlike earlier picture within-a-picture sets I'd seen, with monochrome, coarse, grainy auxiliary images, this proto-type model displayed two full-resolution color pictures.

Panasonic's receiver and other TV models at

the show were the first glimpse given to the
public of the most revolutionary change of
all time. These were digital TV sets—in
effect, sophisticated computers that act as
television receivers.

Notice now, that your television receiver becomes a
complicated computer with an image. Also notice the statement, "Glowing in one corner of the main TV image." Thus,
the image of the beast could be projected in the corner of
your television screen during regular programming at any
and all times.

◆ Here's a description of the ultimate computer from a
secular publication, National Enquirer, December 13, 1983:

A super computer will solve all our
problems—and even crack jokes. The
ultimate computer will look like a giant
robot and act like a human being—making
lightning fast decisions on its own, feeling
human emotions like friendship, and even
making jokes.

There will be one super-brain for the whole
world. Housed in a ten foot-high body, it
will search out and solve mankind's
problems—crime, ill health, bad weather,
traffic jams, etc. That's how futurists like
Saul Kent—author of *The Life-Extension
Revolution* visualizes the ultimate computer
of tomorrow.

"The ultimate computer will not only be
endowed with many human characteristics,
designers will construct it in a humanlike
form so they can treat it as much like a
human as possible," said Kent. It could be a
colossal robot up to ten feet high, and it will
be mobile, able to move itself in case of war.
It will develop traits characteristic of a
human personality.

You can readily see that this giant lifelike robot would be very impressive and, of course, in the beginning it would be helping people. This electronic superhero would be "the good guy" in this end-time scenario. But a colossus with these electronic capabilities could easily become "big brother" watching you, as told in Revelation chapter 13.

The image of the ages, the golden colossus of Nebuchadnezzar's nightmare will become in the last days the ultimate horror story of all time. Like Frankenstein, he comes alive in the Apocalypse of the New Testament (Rev. 13:15) and unleashes carnage and chaos upon a world in total rebellion against God. God's smiting stone, cut without hands (indicating both the eternal nature of the heavenly kingdom and the supernatural nature of the divine son of God) crushes the manmade giant image into powder. This brings a decisive end to all of man's imagery and idolatry:

> Thou sawest till that a stone was cut out without hands, which smote the image upon his feet that were of iron and clay and break them to pieces. Then was the iron, the clay, the brass, the silver, and the gold, broken to pieces together and became like the chaff of the summer threshing floors: and the wind carried them away, that no place was found for them, and the stone that smote the image became a great mountain and filled the whole earth. (Dan. 2:34,35)

So when the image of the ages is no more, the kingdom of Heaven will have come upon earth and the anointed of God, His only son who is the express image of the Father, will reign as King of Kings and Lord of Lords!

> And the seventh angel sounded, and there were great voices in heaven. saying, the kingdoms of this world are become the kingdoms of our Lord, and of His Christ: and He shall reign forever and ever. (Rev. 11:15)

Three

IMITATING THE IMAGE

We live not only in the information age but in the century when media is King. God asked Job, "Hast thou an arm like God? Or canst thou thunder with a voice like Him?" (Job 40:9). Today, man is steadily increasing his influence over this planet, and even reaching out into space by means of incredible technology. He is, as it were, throwing his voice around the world by utilizing the amazing electronic technology of radio and television, satellite and cable. In anticipation of such an incredible age, we note the words of God in Job, "Canst thou send lightnings, that they may go, and say unto thee, here we are?" (Job 38:35).

More and more scientists are confronted with the Thesis, "In the beginning God created the heaven and the earth" (Gen. 1:1). The New Testament further declares, "Through faith we understand that the worlds were framed by the Word of God, so that things which are seen were not made of things which do appear." Man unleashes energy by his scientific knowledge; God does it by the Word of His mouth.

The writer of Hebrews tells us that "the Word of God is quick and powerful, and sharper than any two-edged sword, piercing even to the dividing asunder of soul and spirit, and of the joints and marrow, and is a discerner of the thoughts and intents of the heart" (Heb. 4:12).

Man divides the atom by a formula; God does it by His

voice, "The voice of the Lord divideth the flames of fire" (Ps. 29:7).

Today, man virtually worships unseen energy which makes his life far easier than his forebearers, transports him far and wide at incredible speeds and is the wave of the future in terms of nuclear energy. In fact, President Reagan was so interested in the Superconducting Supercollider that he budgeted 4.4 billion dollars to develop this fifty-three mile circumference particle accelerator.

Here I quote from "Dawn of the New Stone Age." July 1987 *Readers Digest*, page 131 "An Electrifying Discovery":

> Scientists have long dreamed of an everyday superconductor that would carry electricity without the slightest loss. Besides saving billions in transmission costs, such a development could enable nuclear power plants to be located far from urban centers. Superconductors could make possible electric motors one-tenth normal size, high-speed trains levitated by magnets, computers smaller and faster than today's, and magnetic imaging machines inexpensive enough for every doctor's office. Indeed, superconductors could transform technology on a scale unseen since the advent of the transistor.
>
> Until now, superconductivity existed only at temperatures near absolute zero-minus 460 degrees Fahrenheit. But recent discoveries have raised the prospect of super-conductors that could work at room temperature. On January 27, 1986, in Ruschlikon, Switzerland, IBM scientists K. Alex Muller and J. Georg Bednoriz discovered superconductivity in a ceramic made of lanthanum-copper oxide laced with barium.
>
> Since then, by changing the recipe slightly,

other scientists have driven the critical temperature more than 100 degrees above absolute zero. "I believe room temperature is possible," says C. W. Chu of the University of Houston.

Before these breakthroughs, superconductors had to be cooled with liquid helium—worth up to $30 a gallon. The new materials can be cooled by liquid nitrogen, which is cheaper than milk. Scientists urge caution about predicting quick success for the new materials since the materials are ceramics, a highly developed manufacturing technology already exists. "If you could go down to the corner hardware store and say you want wire," says Marvin Cohen a physicist at the University of California at Berkeley "and they would say what kind, normal or superconducting? that would certainly change the world."

In our high-speed generation, man is rapidly uncovering and unleashing the secrets of the universe. Man—apart from God—desires to order his world and echo the ambitions of Lucifer who aspired to be the Most High and create his throne above the stars of God. "For thou hast said in thine heart, I will ascend into heaven. I will exalt my throne above the stars of God: I will sit also upon the mount of the congregation in the sides of the north: I will ascend above the heights of the clouds; I will be like the Most High" (Isa. 14:13,14).

Man, in working to set up a global society, is already worshipping the god of forces or energy. This is the only god, the Antichrist, or willful king of Daniel 11 regards:

> And the king shall do according to his will: and he shall exalt himself and magnify himself above every god, and shall speak marvelous things against the God of gods, and shall prosper till the indignation be

accomplished: for that that is determined
shall be done. (Dan. 11:36-38)

To demonstrate how man is turning back the pages of
time and endeavoring to look upon the world with God-like
eyes, consider one paragraph from *The Mountain Observer*
June 12,1987 on the front page:

> What is the Superconducting Supercollider?
> Physically, it's comprised of a tunnel, about
> 10 feet in diameter that will run in a 52 mile
> circle. The tunnel will house a transporter for
> equipment and personnel, a transporter for
> magnets, and two beam pipes to move and
> accelerate protons to an energy of 20 trillion
> electron volts. Magnets, cooled by liquid
> helium, are needed to bend and focus the
> proton beam on its 52 mile track, hence the
> term *superconducting*. The fact that the
> protons, which began their journey as the
> nuclei of ionized hydrogen atoms in a gas,
> will be extracted and made to collide
> accounts for the second term in the machine:
> *Supercollider*. Several points along the giant
> proton race track will be intersection points
> where detectors will monitor 100 million
> collisions per second. These collisions or
> "events" could open a door to conditions that
> prevailed at the beginning of time and open
> a new era in high energy physics.

Actually the super-conducting Supercollider will require a sixteen thousand acre site with forty-three water
wells and a closed airport and the state that has obtained
this super colossus will reap six thousand new jobs. Notice
that the scientists keep talking about "revealing the secrets
of Creation." Quoting another front page article "Run for the
Money" in the *Albuquerque Journal*, June 21, 1987:

> Ultimately, by spinning atoms around
> inside a tube shaped like an oval doughnut
> and making them move at near the speed of

light, then smashing them together head-on,
the device may solve the mystery of how the
universe was created. In more mundane
terms, what's at stake now is the installation
of the superconducting supercollider, a
concrete tunnel at least 30 feet underground
and shaped in an oval 53 miles around. The
tunnel will house the wiring and the
magnets and the paraphernalia for experiments never before possible. They are so
new, in fact, that at least one scientist has said
he doesn't know exactly what all will result
once the thing is cranked up.

The electronic glue or catalyst that is inter-networking
the mass media is, of course, the fantastic super-computers
of the 1990s. Let me show you how all the pieces are coming
together in the prophetic puzzle; the end-time scenario for
the Antichrist system is being made ready. Quoting *The
Indianapolis Star*, June 14,1987 in an article entitled "Immortality?" the sub-heading reads, "Computerizing Brain Will
Let Mind Live On, Roboticist Says," PITTSBURGH:

If you can survive beyond the next 50 years
or so, you may not have to die at all—at least,
not entirely. That's one vision of the future
being fashioned on the frontier of robotics
and artificial intelligence research, where
many of the nation's experts are talking in
terms once reserved for the wildest science
fiction.

Hans Moravec, director of the Robotics
Institute at Carnegie Mellon University,
believes that computer technology is
advancing so swiftly there is little we can do
to avoid a future world run by superintel-
ligent robots.

Unless, he says, we become them ourselves.

In an astonishingly short amount of time,
scientists will be able to transfer the contents

of a person's mind into a powerful computer, and in the process, make him—or at least his living essence—virtually immortal, Moravec claims.

"The things we are building are our children, the next generation," the burly, 39-year-old scientist says. "They're carrying on all our abilities, only they're doing it better. If you look at it that way, it's not so devastating."

The blond, Austrian-born Moravec laughs giddily—somewhat like a movieland mad scientist—as he expounds on his more bizarre notions. But his ideas are thought chillingly sane by many of his colleagues.

"I have found, in traveling throughout all of the major robotics and artificial intelligence centers in the United States and Japan, that the ideas of Hans Moravec are taken seriously," says Grant Fjermedal, author of *The Tomorrow Makers*, a recent book about the future of computers and robotics.

Along with Stanford University and the Massachusetts Institute of Technology, CMU is considered part of a "holy trinity" of leading American research centers into robotics and artificial—or machine—intelligence, says Fjermedal, who devotes the first five chapters of his book to the work of Moravec and his proteges at CMU.

MIT's Gerald J. Sussman, who wrote the authoritative textbook on artificial intelligence, agreed that computerized immortality for people isn't very long from now. "A machine can last forever, and even if it doesn't, you can always make backups," Sussman told Fjermedal. "I'm afraid, unfortunately, that I'm the last generation to die. Some of my students may manage to survive a little longer."

Moravec's futuristic scenario has already come true on the big screen, as well as the small. In creating Max Headroom, the cyberpunk computer personality who starred in a weekly television series and Coca-Cola commercials, and computer fantasies like the movie TRON, science fiction writers have "picked up on some real possibilities," Moravec says.

"Max Headroom is to the future what Flash Gordon was to space travel," he says. "There was a lot of fantasy, but it was more real than a lot of people gave it credit for." The notion of artificial intelligence also had its detractors, of course, including some of the key researchers who are battling the myriad problems of how to teach machines to think and learn independently, as humans do.

In Moravec's book, *Mind Children,* he argues that economic competition for faster and better information-processing systems is forcing the human race to engineer its own technological Armageddon—one that a nuclear catastrophe can only delay.

Moravec's projections are based on his research showing that, on the average, the cost of computation has halved every two years from the time of the primitive adding machines of the late 19th century to the supercomputers of the 1980s.

"Moreover, the rate is speeding up, and the technological pipeline is full of new developments, like molecule-sized computer circuits and recent advances in superconductors that can sustain the pace for the foreseeable future," he says.

"It is no surprise that studies in artificial intelligence have shown sparse results in the last twenty years," Moravec says. Scientists are severely limited by the calculating speed and capacity of laboratory computers. Today's supercomputers running at full tilt, can match in power only the one-gram brain of a mouse, he says.

"But by the year 2010, assuming the growth rate of the last 80 years continues, the best machines will be a thousand times faster than they are today and equivalent in speed and capacity to the human mind," Moravec argues.

"By 2030, calculating costs will be so much reduced that the average personal computer, by then a powerful thinking robot, could easily be your best friend. There are a number of different scenarios of digitizing the contents of the human mind into a computer, all of which will be made plausible in the next fifty to one hundred years by the race of current technology," Moravec says.

One possibility is to hook up a superpowerful computer to the corpus callosum, the bundle of nerve fibers that connects the two hemisphere of the brain. The computer can be programmed to monitor the traffic between the two and eventually to teach itself to think like the brain.

After a while, the machine begins to insert its own messages into the thought stream. "The computer's coming up with brilliant solutions and they're just popping into your head," Moravec says with a giggle. As you lose your natural brain capacity through aging, the computer takes over, function by function. And with advances in brain scanning, you might not need any messy surgery," Moravec says. "Perhaps you just wear some kind of helmet or headband." At the same time, the person's aging, decrepit body is replaced with robot parts.

"In the long run, there won't be anything left of the original. The person never noticed— his train of thought was never interrupted," he says.

This scenario probably is more than fifty years away, Moravec says, but because breakthroughs in medicine and biotechnology are likely to extend people's life spans, "anybody now living has a ticket."

Like many leading artificial intelligence researchers, Moravec discounts the mind-body problem that has dogged philosophers for centuries: whether a person's iden- tity—in religious terms, his soul can exist independently of the physical brain. "If you can make a machine that contains the contents of your mind, then that machine is you, says MIT's Sussman."

Consider this far-out information in light of the bionic man concept—the beast that received a deadly wound and yet lives and his image that comes alive:

And deceiveth them that dwell in the earth by the means of those miracles which he had power to do in the sight of the beast; saying to them that dwell on the earth, that they should make an image to the beast, which had the wound by a sword, and did live.

And he had power to give life unto the image of the beast, that the image of the beast should both speak and cause that as many as world not worship the image of the beast should be killed." (Rev. 13:14,15)

We live in such a day when all of the bizarre predictions of Revelation are believable and scientifically possible. It seems as we faintly hear the Armageddon drum roll, scientists are walking in step with the Creator who holds the future in the hollow of his hand.

Four

REACHING FOR THE GLOBAL IMAGE
BEYOND BABEL

Man is reaching out to extend his global image and then, by means of his vaunted technology to stretch his dominion into the starry heavens. As an article we quote briefly from the *Wall Street Journal* describes it, "Twentieth century man dreams of moving far beyond the tower of Babel's one-world system of Genesis 11—he wants to conquer the cosmos!"

Man is accelerating his date with destiny, and his time warp treadmill is taking him farther than he has ever been before. The final decade of this century will doubtless usher in the new world order to which mankind aspires and to which the New Age movement vows allegiance. The seventy nations descended from Noah after the great flood, all trace their beginnings from the Middle East—the community called Babel. The Bible's description of this near-perfect setting is recorded in Genesis:

> And the whole earth was of one language, and of one speech. And it came to pass, as they journeyed from the east, that they found a plain in the land of Shinar; and they dwelt there. And they said one to another, Go to, let us make brick, and burn them thoroughly. And they had brick for stone, and slime had they for mortar. And they

> said, go to, let us build us a city and a tower,
> whose top may reach unto heaven; and let
> us make us a name, lest we be scattered
> abroad upon the face of the whole earth.
> (Gen. 11:1-4)

These early Babel builders had the one-world concept and the philosophy of globalists today. They were the original empire builders who desired to build cities and monuments apart from God and immortalize their own names. Some authors have suggested that man is marching back to Babel but in reality, man is endeavoring to throw off all restraint and move far beyond Babel. The prophetic setting is given in one of the psalms: "Why do the heathen rage, and the people imagine a vain thing? The kings of the earth set themselves, and the rulers take counsel together, against the lord, and against His anointed, saying, Let us break their bands asunder, and cast away their cords from us" (Ps. 2:1-3).

Daniel also warns that the Antichrist, in assuming God-like powers, will change times and laws that will result in worldwide catastrophe and upset the balance of nature in this solar system. "And he shall speak great words against the most High, and shall wear out the saints of the most High, and think to change times and laws: and they shall be given into his hand until a time and times and the dividing of time" (Dan. 7:25).

Commenting further on this catastrophe, Isaiah says, "The earth also is defiled under the inhabitants thereof because they have transgressed the laws, changed the ordinance, broken the everlasting covenant. Therefore hath the curse devoured the earth, and they that dwell therein are desolate; therefore the inhabitants of the earth are burned, and few men left" (Isa. 24:5-6).

It seems that science and technology, in opening these windows of wisdom or space windows, have charted an uncertain and possibly chaotic future for this planet. Quoting *Rush To Armageddon* by Texe Marrs, chapter 1, "Who Needs God" on page twenty-three, we read:

It is important to note that many of the world's greatest scientists are Christians. Even among those who do not believe are a number who fear that science and technological progress will lead to widespread abuse and damage to humanity.

In their recent book *The Dehumanization of Man*, Ashley Montagu and Floyd Matson allude to this misuse of science. They find repellent the sexology of psychologists Masters and Johnson, the celebration of violence in movies and punk rock lyrics, mass advertising methods, and television programming. They say that our technological culture is producing a society of "single cheerful robots," cleverly programmed and controlled by technicians who are the masters holding political power.

Many scientists concur with this analysis. In his excellent book *Future Life*, Michel Salomon, a noted French doctor and science editor, interviewed eighteen renowned scientists, six of whom were Nobel Prize winners. Salomon asked each their views of the future and where science might be taking mankind. Their answers were startling.

Erwin Chargaff has been called the "Father of Bioengineering." A "new barbarism" is what he dismally predicts for the future.

I see the beginnings of a new barbarism . . . which tomorrow will be called a "new culture." Naziism was a primitive, brutal, and absurd expression of it. But it was a first draft of the so-called scientific or pre-scientific morality that is being prepared for us in the radiant future.

Chargaff's frightening conclusion is that the world is on the edge of catastrophe, brought about by the abuse of science. "Before every catastrophe," he warned, "as before an earthquake, there are signs of what is to come." The new culture that Chargaff warned about is already quickly taking shape. And just as Chargaff envisioned, the new barbarism comes cloaked with respectability, cleverly disguised as the only rational religion for twenty-first century scientific man.

Another Nobel Prize-winning scientist interviewed by Dr. Saloman was Belgium's Christian deDuve. Echoing Chargaff's fears, deDuve said he was

> convinced that the future is going to find man face to face with some very grave tests—tests that in one way or another will be linked with the abuse of certain kinds of scientific and technical progress . . . For it not to happen, humanity would have to acquire, very rapidly, a heavy dose of wisdom. And today's world would not seem to warrant this happening.

Perhaps the most revealing statement was that of Gabriel Nahaus, world-famous biochemist and researcher, "I believe that twentieth-century man is intoxicated by all the technological conquests that have been made, in particular the conquest of space and the moon landing." "Intoxication"! Is Nahaus correct? Does scientific progress make man drunk with pride and obliterate any and all thoughts of God in his heart? The evidence seems to indicate that it does. Indeed, the evidence tells us that man is beginning to believe in his own omnipotence. Man is coming to believe that he is God. This is exactly what Satan wants mankind to believe.

It is obvious that scientists are more pessimistic than preachers. In spite of all the fantastic achievements in computers, satellites, and nuclear weapons, men of science are still expecting Armageddon rather than the golden age. They are expecting the worst possible consequences from the scientific projects now developing in the laboratories.

The title and information of a secular paid advertisement of AT & T on Telecommunications carried in the *Wall Street Journal* are singularly meaningful:

Issues of the Information Age: THE WAY BEYOND BABEL—Imagine trying to build a railroad system if every locomotive manufacturer used a different track gauge. Every local stretch of railroad had its own code of signals. And in order to ride a train, you needed to know the gauges and the signals and the switching procedures and the route and the conductor's odd pronunciation of the station names.

The business of moving and managing information is in a similar state today. Machines can't always talk to each other. Proprietary systems and networks abound, with suppliers often jockeying to make theirs the de facto standard. The enormous potential of the Information Age is being dissipated by incompatibility.

The solution, as we see it, is common standards, which would allow electronic systems in one or many locations to work together. People will be informed and in control, while the systems exchange, process, and act on information automatically.

AT&T is working with national, international, and industry-wide organizations to set up comprehensive, international standards, to be shared by everyone who uses and provides information technology. We think it's time for everyone in our industry to commit to developing firm, far-reaching standards. The goal: to provide our customers with maximum flexibility and utility. Then, they can decide how and with whom to work.

We foresee a time when the promise of the Information Age will be realized. People will

participate in a worldwide Telecommunity
through a vast global network of networks,
the merging of communications and computers. They'll be able to handle information
in any form—conversation, data, images,
text—as easily as they make a phone call
today.

The science is here now. The technology is
coming along rapidly. But only with
compatibility will the barriers to Telecommunity recede. Telecommunity is our goal.
Technology is our means. We're committed
to leading the way.

It is interesting that industrial giants talk so blithely
about the Information Age, especially in view of Daniel's
special prophecy about the increase of knowledge. "But
thou, 0 Daniel, shut up the words, and seal the book, even
to the time of the end: Many shall run to and fro, and
knowledge shall be increased" (Dan. 12:4).

We have been aware for some months of the current
project to completely modernize the telecommunications in
the Common Market countries and make them compatible.
This system may well be the most sophisticated in the
coming decade, and you can be sure the United States will
be linked up to this coming network of networks. Of course,
the United States has the same fantastic dream of one world,
one wire. This bold blueprint is set forth in a remarkable and
recent article entitled "Rewiring The World" by Mark L.
Goldstein that appeared in *Industry Week*, published June
15,1987, page forty-four. Mark Goldstein asserts that

the dream of a single all-digital communications network is slowly being translated into
reality. Telephones will become smarter,
and voice and data will be transmitted
simultaneously. The first commercial use
could begin next year, though 1995 seems
more likely for the residential market.

Back in the 1950's, President Eisenhower's

bold plan to sew up the nation with super-highways had its critics. They couldn't reconcile the vast capital requirements of the project with the need for four lanes of asphalt across the wheat fields of the Midwest. Detractors said no one would use it.

Today, as America maps out plans for the next decade to overhaul its convoluted, often incompatible communications net-work, doubters are again asking some of the same questions. The massive cost of developing a sophisticated universal net-work able to transmit any combination of voice, data, images, and video anywhere in the nation—eventually the world—leaves many skeptics wondering what good it will do for tomorrow's little old ladies in the hinterlands—forget about who will pay for it.

Yet the project has already begun. Old analog lines are gradually being replaced by digital ones. Long distance companies such as AT & T and U. S. Sprint have sunk more than $8 billion in the last four years into fiber-optic networks. At the same time, the Bell Operating Companies (BOCs), scions of the former Bell System, are starting to upgrade and replace with computerized digital machines the old analog public switches that route millions of phone calls annually.

It's an expensive, complicated process. Only about 20% of all public switches are capable of handling digital calls today, but it's expected that nearly 90% of network switches will be replaced or converted by 1990. And given the recent surge of private network investments by large corporations looking for more capacity and control in their systems, it's not difficult to see why industry analysts are predicting that today's $120 billion communications services market will likely exceed $200 billion by 1990.

ONE WIRE. That's just the first step. For nearly a decade in the U. S., Europe, and Japan, network planners at AT & T and other companies have been working on a road map that takes advantage of new technologies—including digitization and semiconductor advancements—to connect the major communications media into a single, universal system. Called "integrated services digital network" (ISDN), it promises a new era in which virtually all communications equipment, from a plain telephone or personal computer to a full-blown video conference or futuristic videophone, can operate simultaneously through one wire.

Standing on the threshold of the Information Age is like viewing a science fiction movie. It astounds your mental faculties and is only half believable. Not only is our world of technology rushing toward the global system of the twenty-first century man and the new world order, but also the work force is being prepared for the world of tomorrow by New Age seminars on mind control. The world is being prepared technologically and spiritually for the new world order, and man is almost ready to go beyond Babel. Notice the universal mind control that will come upon the world through Satan's man, the Antichrist. The Bible contends:

> For the mystery of iniquity doth already work: only he who now letteth will let, until he be taken out of the way. And then shall that Wicked be revealed, whom the Lord shall consume with the spirit of his mouth and shall destroy with the brightness of his

coming: Even him, whose coming is after the working of Satan with all power and signs and lying wonders. (II Thess. 2:7-9)

Five

IMAGES OF AI
ARTIFICIAL INTELLIGENCE

The Impetus of nations rushing toward their prophetic destiny is likened to "the rushing of mighty waters," by the prophet Isaiah.

> Woe to the multitude of many people, which make a noise like the noise of the seas; and to the rushing of nations, that make a rushing like the rushing of mighty waters! The nations shall rush like the rushing of many waters: but God shall rebuke them, and they shall flee far off, and shall be chased as the chain of the mountains before the wind, and like a rolling thing before the whirlwind. (Isa. 17:12-13)

Notice also that God's whirlwind will scatter and destroy man's best efforts to set up a new world order apart from God. But man desperately wants to create and exercise his god-like powers. Some of man's best work is demonstrated in robotics and fantastic new computers. In quoting Texe Marr's outstanding book, *Rush To Armageddon*, page twenty-seven, chapter 2 "Man the Creator: Robotics and Bioengineering," we read:

> The technologies of bioengineering and robotics are destined to make fantastic changes in our material world. In the science of bioengineering—often called genetic

engineering—more than two hundred companies in the United States alone are working to splice genes and invent new life-forms. Meanwhile, robots have already replaced hundreds of thousands of workers on factory assembly lines. The government's Office of Technology Assessment predicts that as many as one-third of all industrial workers may, by the year 2000, find themselves unemployed—victims of robots and automation. In Japan, we get a glimpse into the future. There, in the city of Fanue, industrial robots toil seven days a week, twenty-four hours a day, building new robots.

Experts in robotics and artificial intelligence are working hard to perfect lifelike robots with silicon chip brains that can think, make independent judgments, and take actions without the assistance of humans. By the year 2000 or shortly thereafter, biological engineering—which has already created bacterial lifeforms in the lab—will wed its knowledge to that of the roboticists. "Biological chips"—fleshly substances—will be used to construct the brains of robots. Several companies are already working on this project.

In his fascinating book *The Intimate Machine: Close Encounters with Computers and Robots*, Englishman Neil Frude says that soon we shall have robots as companions and even as sex partners. This will be made possible by new achievements in robotics technology looming on the horizon, achievements which include the use of materials similar to human flesh and the manufacture of organic "brains" or biological computer units. This is not science fiction malarkey. It is reality.

Stanley Wellborn, in *U.S. News and World Report*, Dec 31, 1984, reported on the biochip revolution, which he called "the race to create a living computer." "Man-made organic computers might be able to detect their own internal design flaws and even repair and replicate themselves. Miniscule computers implanted in the brain could monitor body chemistry and correct imbalances. They could connect with the human nervous system, serving as artificial eyes, ears, and voice boxes . . ."

Robotics is a science that offers wonderful benefits for mankind. But progress in this field and in bioengineering does have potential for harm due to the perversion of Satan. Arthur C. Clarke, world-famous author of *2001:A Space Odyssey*, and numerous other futuristic books, believes that the statement "God made man in His own image" is ticking away like a time bomb at the foundations of Christianity.

Clarke made his remark when asked what would be the effect on civilization if man found extra-terrestrial life on other planets. But what of life created by man here on earth? The introduction of intelligent robots and manmade biological life in the laboratory is already tearing away at the foundations of Christianity. In the thinking of many people, man is divine, mankind is a creator, and God is therefore either nonexistent, irrelevant, impotent, or at best, no more than the equal of man.

Is man creating life in the test tube? Will science be able to ultimately create synthetic life, near-life, or life itself? Apparently, man will succeed in creating some kind of life before God intervenes and brings man to a sudden halt. In terms of worship and control, the basic technology is already being developed to fulfill the end-time scenario.

Solomon tells us that there is "nothing new under the sun," but in terms of lasers and computers, the whole emerging network of telecommunications, change and innovation is the order of the day. Get ready for the New Age, the new world order, the golden age for which man, the creator, has dreamed and worked for long centuries. You will be amazed at some of the things that are already being done in our global society in the area of banking and business.

We read in *Popular Mechanics*, October 1986, page seventy-six, an article by Paul A. Willax entitled, "Cashing In on the Future":

> Lasers and computers loom large in the future of banking. Transactions will be easier, and counterfeiting harder. Less than 40 years ago, at the University of Pennsylvania, an assemblage of 18,000 vacuum tubes, 70,000 resistors, 10,000 capacitors and 6,000 switches—enough gizmos to fill a two car garage—huffed and puffed at highspeed calculations as ENIAC (Electronic Numerical Integrator and Calculator), the granddaddy of the digital calculator, was born. The revolution that followed touched every corner of society, and has already transformed the banking industry from manually entering transactions on ledger cards to electronically moving funds around the globe in a matter of seconds.

> Yet, we've just heard the first rumblings of a revolution that will soon change the face of banking, and money, in ways you may never have imagined. Imagine this: As the Eiffel Tower stands watch over sleepy Paris, an advanced microcomputer, I call the Electronic Pal (EP), maintains a silent vigil on a nightstand in an American

businessman's hotel room. EP scans the Dow-Jones newswire and other financial reports as its owner sleeps. Half a world away, the New York Stock Exchange is ready to end a day of quiet trading when word hits the floor that IBM stocks are splitting. EP, with a large memory processor etched into its tiny chips, reacts to key words in the report. Using artificial intelligence, the key words "split" and "IBM" set it in motion to take constant updates on the situation. EP is talking to the stock exchange supercomputer via a satellite connection. As it monitors those reports, EP automatically switches to another satellite network to talk to the sleeping businessman's home computer.

Having been trained by the businessman to follow his portfolio in a set pattern, EP notes the man's IBM holdings and, at 6:00 am., wakes the owner with a buzz. With one flash of numbers, EP tells him what stock is available. With another flash, EP tells him how much cash he has and where. Money has been transferred, and upon the businessman's approval, a deal will be consummated.

All of the various technologies needed to build this theoretical device are available today. In fact, the Electronic Pal is already under discussion in computer circles. Apple computer's co-founder, Stephen Jobs, has described it as "an incredibly powerful helper."

Satellites and computers linked together to allow the traveler to carry all his assets and the marketplace with him are in the future of banking.

Paul Willax also discusses holograms and new money in *Popular Mechanics* as he continues on the subject of money and electronic banking:

> In today's world, money is already moving as quickly as the people who need it. More people are using automated tellers, banking by phone and banking at home using personal computers. And banks are installing equipment like videodisc systems that allow customers to summon up detailed information on a wide range of financial topics.
>
> Other developments have great potential for automated banking. Seiko, for example recently began offering its three-component Datagraph system linking a specially designed wristwatch to most computers. The system lets you retrieve 2000 characters of data from the watch anywhere and any time.
>
> Epson has recently been showing off a much more powerful device. The RC-20 wrist computer includes 2000 bytes of random access memory and houses a computer chip comparable to those used in many pre-IBM personal computers. With its communications port, the RC-20 can communicate with a desktop computer. Link such hardware to emerging software that creates expert systems and you have the forerunner of my Electronic Pal advanced microcomputer described earlier . . .
>
> Nearly 20 years have passed since Arthur C. Clark gave us *2001:A Space Odyssey*. The incredibly powerful HAL 9000 computer created in that story was thought incapable of error. But a series of glitches turned it into a killer computer. We understand that sen-

sitivities of banking and money will always require looking over our shoulders at a criminal element. But the promise of electronic banking is so great, and the possibilities for security so numerous, that future banking with highly intelligent systems is inevitable.

As scientific man looks beyond Babel, he invariably looks to the heavens—the last frontier to be explored—space. Once again the joint efforts of leading nations are propelling mankind farther and faster into the vast recesses of outer space. Quoting *Europe*, September 1987 (the official publication of the Common Market), page sixteen, entitled "U.S., Europeans Plan Joint Missions in Space," we read:

> European nations, buoyed by the success of the Giotto mission to Halley's Comet last year, are proceeding with an ambitious space program that focuses on close cooperation with the United States. Scientists from the European Space Agency (ESA) are discussing joint missions with the United States—one to Saturn and its moon, Titan, and another to return a sample of an as yet undetermined comet back to Earth. ESA will also be an active participant in the U.S. space station, *Columbus*.

> European and American cooperation will be most evident on the *Cassini* spacecraft mission to the ringed Saturn and its giant moon, Titan, proposed for launch in 1995 and arrival in 2002. The main craft will orbit Saturn while a smaller probe, designed and built by ESA, will land on Titan. The landing will be made more difficult by the fact that scientists do not know if Titan's surface is solid or liquid. "We're still debating what to do after we land," said John Beckman, a *Cassini* mission specialist at the National

Aeronautical and Space Administration's (NASA) Jet Propulsion Laboratory in Pasadena, California. "We don't know whether to construct a lander, a ship or a submarine."

The U.S. and European mishaps and the subsequent launch delays have resulted in closer cooperation between Europe and the Soviet Union, including an unprecedented plan to explore the planet Mars and its moon, Phobos. A number of European countries are scheduled to provide experiments for a pair of Soviet spacecraft that will investigate Phobos in 1989. Set for launch next year, two orbiters will circle the tiny moon while a pair of probes land on the surface and send data and television pictures back to Earth. Each of the main spacecraft will carry identical payloads. When the first mothership arrives at Phobos, it will swoop within 200 feet of the surface, deploy its two probes and rocket up to a safer orbital altitude to conduct its own measurements.

The second mothership would reach the Martian system a month or two later. Should any part of the first mothership's mission fail, the second would be able to fill the void. But if the first mission is successful, the second craft could be diverted to Mars' other moon, Deimos, which is about half the size of Phobos' 10-mile diameter.

Both ESA and the independent French space agency, Centre National d'Etudes Spatiales (CNES), will also take part in a spectacular Soviet plan to send an armada of unmanned craft to the Red Planet. Two launches per year are scheduled in 1992, 1994, and 1996. At least two of these spaceships will deploy

rovers to roam the Martian surface, collect-
ing samples of the planet's soil and then
returning the samples to Earth. Europe will
also be represented on these flights.

Man is frantically trying to unlock every door and
discover all the secrets of the universe. But God will shut
the door when man has overstepped his boundaries, even
as God closed the door to the Ark after Noah and his family
had entered in and shut out all the unbelievers (see Gen.
7:16). God's decree is recorded in the book of Psalms, "The
Heaven, even the heavens, are the Lord's: but the earth hath
He given to the children of men" (Ps. 115:16). And God
further warns rebellious man in the book of Obadiah,
"Though thou exalt thyself as the eagle, and though thou set
thy nest among the stars, thence will I bring thee down, saith
the Lord" (Obad. 1:4).

Six

WAR OF THE IMAGES— BEYOND STAR WARS

Warfare in the realm of the spirit world is just as real as in the dimension of the physical or material world; however, we do not ordinarily see the battles that are raging in the spirit world or comprehend the weapons of such metaphysical conflicts.

Paul, by inspiration of the Holy Ghost, draws aside the shadowy curtain that cloaks the unseen world of spiritual dominion and gives us a brief glimpse of some of the activities in the non-material realm. "We wrestle not against flesh and blood," Paul warns.

> Finally, my brethren, be strong in the Lord, and in the power of his might. Put on the whole armor of God, that ye may be able to stand against the wiles of the devil.
>
> For we wrestle not against flesh and blood, but against principalities, against powers, against the rulers of the darkness of this world, against spiritual wickedness in high places.
>
> Wherefore take unto you the whole armor of God, that ye may be able to withstand in the evil day, and having done all, to stand.
>
> Stand therefore, having your loins girt about with truth, and having on the breastplate of

righteousness; And your feet shod with the preparation of the gospel of peace. (Eph. 6:10-15)

Before the beginning of time, Satan, the arch rebel, has been fighting against God and man, striving to regain his dominion over this solar system and especially planet Earth. We are also given clues in the Old Testament as to the fall of Lucifer, one of the angelic princes, who by transgression became the devil and Satan:

How art thou fallen from heaven, 0 Lucifer, son of the morning! how art thou cut down to the ground, which didst weaken the nations! For thou hast said in thine heart, I will ascend into heaven, I will exalt my throne above the stars of God: I will sit also upon the mount of the congregation, in the sides of the north: I will ascend above the heights of the clouds; I will be like the most High. Yet thou shalt be brought down to hell, to the sides of the pit. (Isa. 14:12-15)

More details concerning the dark and cryptic history of this once bright and shining angelic prince are recorded in the book of Ezekiel:

Thou art the anointed cherub that covereth; and I have set thee so: thou wast upon the holy mountain of God; thou hast walked up and down in the midst of the stones of fire.

Thou was perfect in thy ways from the day that thou was created, till iniquity was found in thee. By the multitude of thy merchandise they have filled the midst of thee with violence, and thou hast sinned; therefore I will cast thee as profane out of the mountain of God: and I will destroy thee, 0 covering cherub, from the midst of the stones of fire.

Thine heart was lifted up because of thy

beauty, thou hast corrupted thy wisdom by
reason of thy brightness: I will cast thee to
the ground, I will lay thee before kings, that
they may behold thee.

Thou hast defiled thy sanctuaries by the
multitude of thine iniquities, by the iniquity
of thy trafick; therefore will I bring forth a
fire from the midst of thee, it shall devour
thee, and I will bring thee to ashes upon the
earth in the sight of all them that behold thee.
All they that know thee among the people
shall be astonished at thee: thou shalt be a
terror, and never shalt thou be any more.
(Isa. 14:12-15)

We have still another picture of the traffic in the heavens
and the alien battles that rage in high places, in the appearance of the messenger of the covenant to show Daniel
things that will surely come to pass:

Then said he unto me, Fear not, Daniel: for
from the first day that thou didst set thine
heart to understand, and to chasten thyself
before thy god, thy words were heard, and I
am come for thy words.

But the prince of the kingdom of Persia
withstood me one and twenty days: but, to
Michael, one of the chief princes, came to
help me; and I remained there with the kings
of Persia.

Now I am come to make thee understand
what shall befall thy people in the latter
days: for yet the vision is for many days.

Then said he, Knowest thou wherefore I
come unto thee? And now will I return to
fight with the prince of Persia: and when I
am gone forth, lo, the prince of Grecia shall
come.

But I will show thee that which is noted in

> the scripture of truth: and there is none that
> holdeth with me in these things, but Michael
> your prince. (Dan. 10:12-14,20-21)

Evidently these fallen angelic princes dominated empires and nations from heavenly principalities and guarded their territories jealously against God's messengers. Here, notice the words of Jesus concerning the heavens, when the wicked forces under the devil's dominion (The prince of the power of the air. Eph. 2:2), evidently, realized that the incarnation of Christ would soon take place. "And from the days of John the Baptist until now the kingdom of heaven suffereth violence, and the violent take it by force" (Matt. 11:12).

A notable event in the life of Elisha the prophet illustrates how God sends His warrior angels to protect His servants. Apparently, these spirit beings are invisible to the human eye unless God wants them to be seen:

> Then the King of Syria warred against Israel
> and took counsel with his servants, saying,
> In such and such a place shall be my camp.
> And the man of God sent unto the king of
> Israel, saying, Beware that thou pass not
> such a place; for thither the Syrians are come
> down.
>
> And the king of Israel sent to the place which
> the man of God told him and warned him of
> and saved himself there, not once nor twice.
>
> Therefore the heart of the king of Syria was
> sore troubled for this thing; and he called his
> servants, and said unto them, Will ye not
> shew me which of us is for the king of Israel?
>
> And one of his servants said, None, my lord,
> 0 king: but Elisha, the prophet that is in
> Israel, telleth the king of Israel the words that
> thou speakest in thy bedchamber.
>
> And he said, Go and spy where he is, that I

may send and fetch him. And it was told him, saying, Behold, he is in Dothon.

Therefore sent he thither horses, and chariots, and a great host: and they came by night, and compassed the city about.

And when the servant of the man of God was risen early, and gone forth, behold, an host compassed the city both with horses and chariots. And his servant said unto him, Alas, my master! how shall we do?

And he answered, Fear not; for they that be with us are more than they that be with them. And Elisha prayed, and said, Lord, I pray thee, open his eyes, that he may see. And the Lord opened the eyes of the young man; and he saw: and behold, the mountain was full of horses and chariots of fire round about Elisha.

And when they came down to him, Elisha prayed unto the Lord, and said, Smite this people, I pray thee, with blindness. And he smote them with blindness according to the word of Elisha.

And Elisha said unto them, This is not the way, neither is this the city: follow me, and I will bring you to the man whom ye seek. But he led them to Samaria.

And it came to pass, when they were come into Samaria, that Elisha said, Lord, open the eyes of these men, that they may see. And the Lord opened their eyes, and they saw; and, behold, they were in the midst of Samaria.

And the king of Israel said unto Elisha, when he saw them, My father, shall I smite them? shall I smite them?

And he answered, Thou shalt not smite them, wouldest thou smite those whom thou hast taken captive with thy sword and with thy bow? Set bread and water before them, that they may eat and drink, and go to their master.

And he prepared great provision for them: and when they had eaten and drunk, he sent them away, and they went to their master. So the bands of Syria came no more into the land of Israel. (II Kings 6:8-23)

The Bible tells us that war will break out in the heavens during the seven years of tribulation. Today we see the superpowers preparing for war in the heavens and a star wars defense in outer space. There is little doubt that World War III will be fought in outer space as well as on this planet. The Bible describes the tribulation war in the heavens and the decisive result:

And there was war in heaven; Michael and his angels fought against the dragon; and the dragon fought and his angels, And prevailed not; neither was their place found any more in heaven.

And the great dragon was cast out, that old serpent, called the Devil, and Satan, which deceiveth the whole world: he was cast out into the earth, and his angels were cast out with him. (Rev. 12:7-9)

Since 1983, the United States has been talking about the need for a Star Wars or Strategic Defense Initiative program. Apparently, the Russians have been working on a Star Wars defense for more than ten years. However, there is a more fearful and awesome possibility, and this is thoroughly and categorically discussed in a book by Lt. Col-ret Archibald L. Roberts. The credits for the book carried in the "Bulletin" are as follows:

Soviet Scalar Electromagnetic Weapons, review of a book by Thomas E. Bearden, Lt Col, AUS, ret, P O Box 1472, Huntsville, AL

35807, begins on this page. The astounding
works of Colonel Bearden, nuclear engineer,
war games analyst, and military tactician
with over 26 years experience in air defense
systems, tactics and operations, technical
intelligence, anti-radiation missile counter-
measures, nuclear weapons employment,
computerized war games and military
systems requirements, have been previously
reported in the CRC BULLETIN: The Tesla
Factor, Free Energy, End of Nuclear Race
Possible Through New-age Science
(November 1984), and, Star Wars Now,
Secret Soviet Tesla Weapons Doom Budget-
busting U. S. Defense System (April 1985).

In this dynamic book, we learn that Russian scientists
have for many years been working and experimenting with
Tesla's secrets. The results of these highly technical tests
may have caused the explosion at Chernobyl and the loss of
American planes, rockets, and submarines over a period of
twenty-five years.

Now quoting portions of *Fer-De-Lance Briefing: SOVIET
SCALAR ELECTROMAGNETIC WEAPONS*:

For over three decades, the Soviet Union has
been developing, deploying, and testing
new scalar electromagnetic (electrogravitational) weapons which up to now have not
been understood by Western scientists.
These weapons are so powerful that, as
Khrushchev stated in 1960, they could
destroy all life on earth if unrestrainedly
used. After nearly twenty years of Soviet
testing, in 1975 Brezhnev revealed that these
weapons were more frightful than the mind
of man had ever imagined, and strongly
urged that their development be banned. In
the same year, Gromyko introduced to the
United Nations a draft agreement for

banning their development and called upon all the nations of the world to sign it.

Fer-De-Lance presents the basic concepts of these frightful Soviet super weapons. Some of the major types available, the startling nature of their effects, and evidence of their widespread testing by the Soviet Union are discussed below:

> The principles for converting electromagnetic energy into gravitational energy, and vice versa, are explained in detail. Scalar EM devices allow creating energy at a distance (Tesla's wireless transmission of energy without loss), extracting energy from a distant point (a cold explosion, such as the one off the coast of Japan on April 9, 1984), exploding nuclear weapons in their silos and storage sites, adding electromagnetic circuits, detecting and destroying underwater nuclear submarines, providing a 100% defense against missiles and bombers, and seeing through the earth or ocean (Tesla's "big eye that can see at a distance").

> The author introduces startling evidence that the Soviet Union has deliberately used these weapons to shoot down Francis Gary Powers' U-2 aircraft in 1960, destroy the *U.S.S. Thresher* atomic submarine in 1963, and engineer the weather over North America since 1975. The Soviets have continued to commit acts of war against the U.S., using giant scalar EM weapons to actually destroy aircraft and missiles over the U.S. and kill American citizens.

> Startling new evidence of Soviet weapons testing against NASA shuttle and missile launches and U.S. airlines is presented. The author contends that the Soviet Union deliberately destroyed the *Arrow DC-8* on

December 12, 1985, killing over 250 Americans. He also contends that the Soviet Union destroyed the *Challenger* space shuttle on January 28, 1986, the *Titan 34D* missile launch on April 18,1986, and the *Delta* rocket on May 3, 1986, virtually paralyzing the U.S. space program. Further, he tells exactly how they did it in each case.

Soviet testing of a scalar EM "death ray" in Afghanistan is revealed. Instant and total death of all body cells results from a strike of the weapon, and the dead body does not decay for an extended period.

Only the supernatural weapons of Almighty God will defeat the great armies of Gog and Magog. These weapons are described in Ezekiel:

And I will call for a sword against him throughout all my mountains, saith the Lord God: every man's sword shall be against his brother. And I will plead against him with pestilence and with blood; and I will rain upon him, and upon his bands, and upon the many people that are with him, an overflowing rain, and great hailstones, fire, and brimstone. (Ezek. 38:21-22)

Continuing to quote *Fer-De-Lance Briefing*,

The reader is introduced to the bizarre world of computer software "worms" and "viruses" and antidotes against them. The eery potential for use of scalar EM "worms" and "viruses" against the brain's own "software" is presented. The startling potential that even one's personality itself can be erased or changed is presented. The potential use of scalar EM for creating death and disease in entire populations is advanced.

An incredible and unsuspected threat to all

humanity, posed by nuclear arms and nuclear facilities struck by scalar EM pulses, is presented for the first time. The author explains how a scalar EM transmitted failure can dump an enormous electrogravitational pulse into the earth, triggering the nearest nuclear material into a sudden burst of radiation. The Kyshtym disaster in 1957 near the Urals and the Chernobyl reactor accident in 1986 were probably triggered by failures of giant scalar EM transmitters nearby.

The terrible judgments of the tribulation period will be both manmade and God-mandated. Observe the results of God's vials of wrath:

> And I heard a great voice out of the temple saying to the seven angels, Go your ways, and pour out the vials of the wrath of God upon the earth
>
> And the first went, and poured out his vial upon the earth, and there fell a noisome and grievous sore upon the men which had the mark of the beast, and upon them which worshiped his image.
>
> And the second angel poured out his vial upon the sea; and it became as the blood of a dead man: and every living soul died in the sea. (Rev. 16:1-3)

He continues:

> And the fourth angel poured out his vial upon the sun; and power was given unto him to scorch men with fire.
>
> And men were scorched with great heat, and blasphemed the name of God, which hath power over these plagues: and they repented not to give him glory. (Rev. 16:8-9)

The scalar EM linkage between the earth, sun, and moon is detailed. The bizarre danger of inadvertently and catastrophically initiating giant scalar resonances of the sun and moon by use of large scalar weapons is detailed. Seismic convulsions of the mantle, giant tidal waves, and a rain of fire from the sun could all be initiated by accident.

The potentially outer-space resonances could be the result described in the book of Joel:

> And I will shew wonders in the heavens and in the earth, blood, and fire, and pillars of smoke. The sun shall be turned into darkness, and the moon into blood, before the great and the terrible day of the Lord come. (Joel 2:30, 31)

And also in the book of Isaiah:

> Moreover the light of the moon shall be as the light of the sun, and the light of the sun shall be sevenfold, as the light of seven days, in the day that the Lord bindeth up the breach of his people, and healeth the stroke of their wound. (Isa. 30:26)

We present the final quote by Col. Bearden:

> The author urges that the U.S. develop scalar EM defenses at utmost speed, and then reach an agreement with the Soviet Union restricting use of these weapons. He points out, however, that soon many other nations—even the despotic—will be able to have powerful scalar EM weapons, and this spells the end of humanity unless positive steps are taken to prevent its destruction.

Only God's direct intervention will prevent the complete destruction of this planet:

> And the nations were angry, and thy wrath is come, and the time of the dead, that they should be judged, and that thou shouldest give reward unto thy servants the prophets, and to the saints, and them that fear thy name, small and great; and shouldest

destroy them which destroy the earth. (Rev. 11:18)

Seven

MAN'S IMAGE IN SPACE

Since the beginning of the space race, man has been looking out into the heavens with greater interest and intensity. He is opening space windows on an accelerating timetable and looking farther into space than ever before. Man is accomplishing these marvels through scientific technology, i.e., radio telescopes, space cameras, and rotating satellites. He is trying to extend his image to outer space.

God's word indicates that the windows in heaven will be open during the last days. "And it shall come to pass, that he who fleeth from the noise of the fear shall fall into the pit; and he that cometh up out of the midst of the pit shall be taken in the snare: for the windows from on high are open, and the foundations of the earth do shake" (Isa. 24:18).

Notice also that activity in the heavens is associated with the shaking of the foundations of the earth—earthquakes. Man is also today working tirelessly to predict days before the devastating tremors of great earthquakes. An illuminating article appeared in *Europe Magazine*, July–August 1988, page six:

> In his home in the seaside suburb of Glyfada, Panayiotis Varotsos has a room filled with seismographic equipment that is linked by computer and telephone to a network of buried electrodes around the country. It is monitored around the clock by Varotsos, an Athens University physics professor, and a

scientific team whose aim is to give reliable warnings of earthquakes in Greece a few days before they are likely to hit.

The VAN earthquake prediction system has been in place for five years and has generally triggered curiosity mixed with skepticism on the part of seismologists abroad. But when Varotsos and his team recently successfully forecast the timing, strength and epicenter of several tremors in the Ionian seabed off western Greece, the results brought renewed interest in the method, and the Greek government now seems likely to increase its funding of the project so that Varotsos' network of 18 scattered monitoring stations can be enlarged.

The system works by tracking electrical impulses emitted from the Earth by means of sensors inserted six feet beneath the ground that are linked to a microcomputer through an amplifier and a telephone line. At Varotsos' home, the scientists keep watch for any variations in the electrical field caused by subterranean stresses that would indicate the building of an earthquake.

The "time-window", as Varotsos calls the lag between the electrical field variations and the actual earthquake, ranges anywhere between seven hours and one week, although the tremor is usually felt within a period of 45 hours to 60 hours.

That proved to be the case with the May and June earthquakes off the island of Cephalonia. Varotsos and his team gave more than two days' warning of three tremors measuring 5.8, 5.3 and 5.0 on the Richter scale at a distance of around 190 miles from Athens. The warnings were

given on the basis of data gathered from a
monitoring station near Ionnina, over 100
miles from the epicenter of the tremors. "It
was the most convincing result of our work
so far. And if we were to expand our
monitoring network to some 40 stations, I
think we could produce many more such
reliable warnings," Varotsos said.

Greece is the most seismically active country
in Europe. Giving birth to more than half the
tremors recorded across the Continent every
year, some 25,000 earthquakes of more than
2 on the Richter scale are logged annually,
while around 250 measure more than 4 on
the Richter scale—the strength at which
cracks start appearing in buildings. Two or
three of them reach 6 Richter every year,
while a potentially disastrous quake of 7
Richter is likely to occur every four years.

But as man avidly peers through time windows, space
windows, and others, frantically trying to unlock God's
secrets, God says concerning the last days: "Whose voice
then shook the earth: but now He hath promised, saying,
yet once more I shake not the earth only, but also heaven"
(Heb. 12:26). Scientists now know that our home planet is
not as stable as it appeared to be; and its observable erratic
wobble seems to be more pronounced. Quoting *Science
News*, July 16, 1988, page thirty-nine "As the World
Wobbles":

The earth seems as stable as the weather is
changeable, but in fact scientists have long
known that movements of air masses can
make the planet wobble on its axis for
periods of a year or more. Now, researchers
using very sensitive satellite and radio
astronomy techniques have found "rapid"
wobbling of the earth on a time scale of two
weeks to several months, and have shown

that the wobbling is at least partially caused by atmospheric changes.

When high and low pressure air masses move about the earth, the weight distribution of the atmosphere is changed. This can make the rotating earth wobble, just as moving the balancing weights on the wheel of a car can change the way the hub rotates. The effect was anticipated in 1862 by Lord Kelvin and has since been observed to at least partially cause the earth's annual wobble and the 14-month Chandler wobble.

The group obtained highly accurate measurements of the earth's movement with a technique called satellite laser ranging, which involves bouncing laser beams off the moon and/or an artificial satellite and measuring the time it takes to travel the distance there and back. They confirmed this information with very long baseline interferometry, in which a number of radiotelescopes on different continents observe a quasar at the same time and compare the signals to get information about the relative motion of the observatories.

Using these techniques, the scientists were able to observe the earth's axis of rotation moving 6 to 60 centimeters over these shorter points.

Does God's Word indicate that catastrophic changes will occur in the earth's rotation in the last days? It certainly does! Isaiah asserts that

> the Lord maketh the earth empty, and maketh it waste, and turneth it upside down, and scattereth abroad the inhabitants thereof. The earth is utterly broken down, the earth is clean dissolved, the earth is moved exceedingly. The earth shall reel to

and fro like a drunkard, and shall be
removed like a cottage; and the transgression thereof shall be heavy upon it; and it
shall fall, and not rise again. (Isa. 24:1,19,20)

It now appears that after a two year moratorium on our
space reversals and failures, the United States is about ready
to go full speed ahead on our space program. This time,
however, the "private sector" will be involved. Here's an
update from *Science News*, July 9, 1988.

The first schedule of planned satellite flights
that private space launching companies will
orbit, released last week, is being hailed in
some quarters as a new phase in the U.S.
space program. . . . Historically, NASA has
handled all commercial space launches in
the United States, but in a major policy
change, DOT is now responsible for
licensing all launches of satellites whose
owners . . . hire commercial companies to
orbit their craft with expendable rockets
fired from U.S. sites. The newly announced
commercial launch schedule, or manifest,
reflects President Reagan's January national
space policy statement, which calls both for
eliminating government launch competition
with the private sector and for avoiding
unnecessary use of the space shuttle's
human crews for launchings. The first
version of the manifest, which so far extends
through May of 1992, represents 18 licenses
for satellite launchings and two for sounding rockets. Topping the list is India's
INSTAT 1-D communication-and-meteorol-
ogy satellite, to be launched next March by
McDonnell Douglas atop one of its *Delta*
rockets. The manifest lists nine U.S.
launchings, among which are the German
ROSAT X-ray telescope and NASA'S
Extreme Ultraviolet Explorer satellite (both

formerly planned as launches by the
shuttle), as well as the *Combined Release and
Radiation Effects Satellite* for NASA and the
Defense Department. Also included are
three *GEOS* weather-watchers for the
National Oceanic and Atmospheric
Administration, a Navy communications
satellite and the two sounding rockets, to
carry microgravity experiments. The other
entries, though also being launched by U. S.
companies, are all communications satellites
for foreign or international customers . . ."

In spite of all man's achievements in outer space, God
will shut the door in the final analysis and bring man back
in judgment. "Though they dig into hell, thence shall mine
hand take them; though they climb up to heaven, thence will
I bring them down" (Amos 9:2). Until two years ago, the
United States was solidly in the lead in the space race. Since
then, Russia has not only overtaken the United States in
space exploration, but according to recent reports, they are
preparing to forge far ahead of us. Quoting *U.S. News and
World Report*, May 16, 1988 "RED STAR RISING," page
forty-eight:

While the U. S. Space program flounders, a
Soviet rocket lifts off every four days—
another step toward commercial and
military dominance of the heavens. Like a
giant winged insect clinging to a stout post,
the space shuttle hangs on the side of the
world's most powerful rocket. The stocky,
delta-wing silhouette is familiar. The location—Baikonur Cosmodrome in Central
Asia—is not. A launch is expected to come
within months, perhaps even during Ronald
Reagan's visit to Moscow in late May. With
the American shuttle still grounded nearly 2
1/2 years after the *Challenger* accident, there
is no more telling symbol than the Soviets'
Kosmolyet ("Space Flyer") of how the steady,

even plodding, march of the Soviet space program has begun to carry the day.

Kosmolyet is expected to fly into orbit, then return to land automatically on a long runway stretching across the Asian desert. If the unmanned flight is a success, cosmonauts Igor Yolk and Anatoly Levchenko will pilot the shuttle in an Earth-orbit mission next year—and the Soviets will have taken another big step in their relentless march on the heavens.

The steps are coming faster and faster these days. The Soviets have taken a lead in manned space flight, in launch rate and in heavy-lift launchers. And the implications for both the U. S. and the Soviet Union go far beyond questions of national prestige. Unlike the race to the moon in the 1960s, the stakes this time are critical. The nation that builds a reliable space-transportation system—and that masters the arduous task of living and working in space—will have an edge in the growing commercial competition over everything from launch services to space manufacturing. And a nation that can quickly launch reconnaissance and communications satellites in a crisis will have an edge in a military competition that increasingly depends upon space to fight a war on the ground.

In the unlikely event of a major war, the Soviet Union's robust space program would provide a clear military advantage. The military apparatus of both the United States and the Soviet Union would be struck blind and dumb if space-based systems were knocked out in a conflict. But the Soviet Union, with three major spaceports—possibly supplemented by mobile launch facilities—could quickly replace any satellites that were destroyed. The U.S., by contrast, is still struggling to get the shuttle flying again and to rebuild its nearly abandoned expendable rocket fleet. The explosion last week in Henderson, Nevada, that destroyed one of only two plants in the country that make a shuttle-fuel component will not help. Last year, the U.S. had eight launches. The Soviets had 95.

The Soviets' lead in heavy-lift launchers was solidified last year with their test of the *Energia*, a massive rocket with four times the payload of the U. S. shuttle. The Energia will carry the Soviet shuttle; it could also launch a space station, a mission to Mars—or the heavy components that would be needed for a *Star Wars* defense system. While the U. S. military has been pushing for a heavy-lift vehicle for years, there's not even a design yet.

Even the pride of the U. S. military space fleet, the photo-reconnaissance satellites that are so powerful they can count the number of people in a crowd, may not be adequate to the tasks ahead. Senator David Boren (D-Ok.) chairman of the Select Committee on Intelligence, is lobbying for an upgrade in the U. S. "national technical means"—spookspeak for spy satellites—if the U. S. is to verify a future strategic-arms treaty.

However, for the troubled U. S. space program, 1991 could be a triumphant year. Again quoting *U.S. News and World Report* (1989) from (pages 50 and 51 an article entitled "America's Long Road Back":

When the space shuttle *Discovery* is launched in August—though continuing glitches may cause that date to slip to September—the

American space program will take off once again. Major science missions, on hold since 1986, are scheduled to go off over the next two years. The $1.4 billion Hubble Space Telescope—which NASA space-science chief Samuel Keller calls "the most important scientific instrument that has ever been built" will allow astronomers to see seven times farther out into the universe than any orbit, tended periodically by shuttle visits, for up to 20 years. The Galileo mission, scheduled to be launched in October, 1989, will visit several of Jupiter's far-off moons for the first time. And *Magellan* will set out to conduct an extensive survey of Venus' surface.

Finding a focus. More important for the long term, the American space program finally has a focus that it lacked for the past decade and a half. President Reagan in February laid out a comprehensive outline to foster commercial operations, develop a permanently manned space station and explore the solar system.

As a crucial first step, the federal government has taken itself out of the commercial-space freight business. No longer will everything be carried up by shuttles; they will fill the more specialized role of carrying people and the larger military and scientific payloads. Privately owned expendable rockets will haul for all-profit payloads, such as communications satellites. The business is already under way: McDonnell Douglas, Martin Marietta and General Dynamics so far have firm contracts worth $770 million to launch 11 satellites for commercial customers plus three weather satellites for NASA.

The initial piece of the American space station—already scaled down and slipped a year by budget constraints—is now scheduled for launch in 1995. If the shuttles are fully operational by then and can deliver crew quarters and laboratory modules on schedule, astronauts will take up permanent residence in late 1996.

The *Star Wars* films may prove to be more prophetic than anyone has ever dreamed. Revelation 12:7-9 indicates there will be all out war in heaven during the time of tribulation. You can be sure that if we do not have a Star Wars defense in outer space, Russia will!

However, there are other heavenly signs that indicate we are living in the last days. Jesus said that just prior to His second advent we should expect signs in the "sun," the "moon," and the "stars." Luke observes that

> there shall be signs in the sun, and in the moon, and in the stars; and upon the earth distress of nations, with perplexity; the sea and the waves roaring; Men's hearts failing them for fear, and for looking after those things which are coming on the earth: for the powers of heaven shall be shaken. And then shall they see the son of man coming in a cloud with power and great glory. And when these things begin to come to pass, then look up, and lift up your heads; for your redemption draweth nigh. (Luke 21:25-28)

Concerning the sun, the Word of God does not leave us in ignorance as to what these signs will be like.

1. Isaiah prophesied: ". . . the light of the sun shall be sevenfold, as the light of seven days" (Isa. 30:26).

2. Joel prophesied: "The sun shall be turned into darkness . . . before the great and terrible day of the Lord come" (Joel 2:31).

3. Jesus prophesied: "Immediately after the tribulation of those days shall the sun be darkened" (Matt. 24:29).

4. John, by revelation, prophesied: ". . . the fourth angel poured out his vial upon the sun . . . ,and men were scorched with great heat . . . (Rev. 16:8-9).

Our sun, a relatively small star, by the process of atomic fusion, is an energy-producing instrument. It was made by the Creator for a particular job, which it has been performing since Creation. When instrument producers of energy can no longer export the same amount they generate, something has to give. In the case of stars, they either blow up (supernova), or they suffer an internal atomic collapse (nova). Novas and supernovas are occurring all the time, with approximately thirty observed each year in our galaxy alone.

That God positioned our sun—a medium-sized star—at just the right place to sustain life as we know it on this planet is a well-known principle of science. However, scientific investigation is already revealing unusual characteristics about our sun. Quoting *Science News*, July 2, 1988, page eight from an article entitled "*New Pictures of the Sun Reveal a Number of Surprising and Puzzling Solar Features*":

> Of average mass, build and appearance, the sun doesn't have much to distinguish it from untold numbers of other stars. In fact, many astronomers think of the sun as a commonplace star, even a dull one. "Nonetheless," says astrophysicist Juri Toomre of the University of Colorado in Boulder, "it has a variety of startling features."
>
> For one thing, as the sun spins on its axis, a point near the equator takes about 25 days to make a round trip, while a point in a polar region requires 33 days to complete a rotation. Moreover, some observations hint the sun's core may be rotating as much as three times faster than its surface. No one has yet developed a theory that fully accounts for these unusual motions.
>
> The sun also reverses and rebuilds its

magnetic field every 11 years or so. Sunspots—dark blemishes that periodically appear and disappear on the sun's face— mark sites of intense magnetic activity. Their strong magnetic fields block or redirect the normal flow of hot gases to the sun's surface. "But we still don't know what actually causes sunspots," says J. W. Harvey of the National Solar Observatory in Tucson, Arizona.

In addition, the sun quivers and shakes. Like a bell, it resonates at specific frequencies, displaying a characteristic acoustic signature. Its surface shows complex patterns of pulsating bulges and depressions produced by a mix of sound waves generated by turbulence at various depths within. Scientists are just beginning to translate these patterns into information about the sun's interior.

Perhaps the sun's most distinctive feature is that it's only about ninety-three million miles from earth. No other star is so readily accessible to earth-based observers. No other star has such a direct influence on the earth's climate and environment. Even tiny variations in brightness could shift climatic patterns, initiating an ice age or prompting a global ice melt.

During the last decade, the arrival of ever-more-sophisticated instruments and techniques for observing the sun has transformed the discipline. Now, solar physics encompasses much more than counting and mapping sunspots, although that remains an important pursuit. From earth, researchers can track subtle movements of the sun's vast surface-movements slower than an idler's leisurely stroll. They can detect streams of

charged particles heated to one million C or
pick out the one lithium atom hidden among
100 billion hydrogen atoms.

The prophecies of Isaiah, Joel, John, and our Lord certainly appear to compositely describe a nova condition of
our sun in the last days in which our sun becomes seven
times hotter and brighter than normal and after seven to
fourteen days collapses and goes dark. That the countdown
for such a cataclysm has already begun could be implied
from additional information given in the *Science News*
article. Again quoting:

> Why the sun seems brighter with more
> sunspots puzzles solar scientists. Says
> Hudson, "Theoretically, this is hard to un-
> derstand right now." One possibility is a
> subtle connection between the sun's pulsa-
> tions and its magnetic activity, which in turn
> could affect luminosity.

> The sun is rapidly approaching a maximum
> in its current sunspot cycle, which could
> come as early as the end of 1989. Researchers
> know from sunspot patterns already
> observed that it will be quite large in terms
> of activity and numbers of sunspots. Some
> of the most active cycles on record have
> occurred within the last 30 or 40 years.

Apocalyptic judgments are also associated with the sun
during the time of great tribulation. Notice what is said in
the book of Revelation:

> And the fourth angel sounded, and the third
> part of the sun was smitten, and the third
> part of the moon, and the third part of the
> stars; so as the third part of them was
> darkened, and the day shone not for a third
> part of it, and the night likewise. (Rev. 8:12)

And also:

> The fourth angel poured out his vial upon

the sun; and power was given unto him to scorch men with fire. And men were scorched with great heat, and blasphemed the name of God, which hath power over these plagues; and they repented not to give him glory. (Rev. 16:8,9)

And finally, the time spoken of in the book of Revelation, when the seas become as the blood of a dead man and the rivers also turn red with putrefying fish, seems to be just around the corner according to reports in the secular press. Quoting *Prophecy in the News*, "RED TIDE...WORLDWIDE" July 1988, page two:

> The condition is called red tide. From time to time, it discolors ocean waters in various places around the world. It is always referred to as red, though waters affected by it may be shaded from yellow through red, through brown. Such tides are poison, both to marine animals and to humans. They kill fish and crustaceans by the millions, and they sicken thousands of swimmers, sometimes with a seriousness that results in death. Needless to say, when they occur, they devastate aquatic industries, such as fishing and tourism. In the past few years they have dramatically increased in scope and intensity. And though scientists are working at top speed, they have no idea why this latest blight on the face of our planet has come about.
>
> Red tides are caused by little-understood forms of algae that can remain in dormant forms for years, patiently waiting for the right conditions before they bloom forth into their mature form. They produce dead and putrid waters, littered with the floating bodies of poisoned sea creatures.
>
> In the "Science Times" section of the May 3,

1988 *New York Times*, a gloomy report was given on the amazing recent proliferation of red tides. Marine biologists quoted in the article are pessimistic about being able to solve the problem. "We are seeing a global first-order change." warned Theodore J. Smayda, a professor of oceanography at the University of Rhode Island.

Stressing that there appears to be a long-term degradation of coastal waters, Virginia K. Tippie, director of estuarine programs for the National Oceanic and Atmospheric Administration said, "If the natural environmental conditions are in the right sequence this year, we will continue to see some problems as we did last year."

In a scientific paper delivered at a symposium last year in Japan, Donald M. Anderson, an associate scientist at the Woods Hole Oceanographic Institution in Massachusetts, said that over the last two decades, scientists have seen "a global increase in the frequency, magnitude and geographic extent" of red tides.

Interviewed by the *Times*, Dr. Anderson said, "There's no question that the toxic species have been more noticeable recently. But there is no way to really quantify what is going on. We have a general view over time that accumulates, but there is no doubt that in certain parts of the world, we are seeing more of these toxic events."

Scientists can only stand by and watch as the red tides continue to bloom with increasing frequency and intensity. Their guesses about the most likely cause of this blight range from increasing pollution to long-range weather changes . . . even to acid rain. But no

one is sure. Their only certainty is that the
condition is rapidly growing worse.

This toxic condition could be the beginning of apocalyptic events so graphically described for us in the Bible. "And
the second angel sounded, and as it were a great mountain
burning with fire was cast into the sea; and the third part of
the sea became blood; And the third part of the creatures
which were in the sea, and had life, died; and the third part
of the ships were destroyed" (Rev. 8:8,9). And again: "The
second angel poured out his vial upon the sea; and it became
as the blood of a dead man; and every living soul died in
the sea."

Evidently, activities in the heavens bring forth resultant
events in the earth. So just as man is polluting both the
heavens and the earth; man's image in the heavens will
hasten the judgment of Almighty God upon this planet and
will cause destruction to engulf this earth as well as outer-
space.

Sin will be decisively judged, and man's image in space
will doubtless usher in the "Day of the Lord" that will
culminate with new heavens and a new earth.

> But the day of the Lord will come as a thief
> in the night; in which the heavens shall pass
> away with a great noise, and the elements
> shall melt with fervent heat, the earth also
> and the works that are therein shall be
> burned up. Seeing then that all these things
> shall be dissolved, what manner of persons
> ought ye to be in all holy conversation and
> godliness, Looking for and hasting unto the
> coming of the day of God, wherein the
> heavens being on fire shall be dissolved, and
> the elements shall melt with fervent heat?
> Nevertheless we, according to his promise,
> look for new heavens and a new earth,
> wherein dwelleth righteousness. (2 Pet.
> 3:10-13)

Eight

ARMAGEDDON'S IMAGE

The world of the tribulation period, that ultimately produces Armageddon, will cause the Dark Ages to appear bright and bland by comparison. As technology builds a global village, bound together by the cords or wires of man's invention, we can almost see the shadowy outline of marching robots inter-connected to the master robot or image of the beast (See Rev. 13:15). Such a world is far more frightening than George Orwell's 1984. As you will note in this revealing chapter, the technology is virtually in man's grasp, and this generation is traveling ever faster on the doomsday train to Armageddon.

Computers and robotics have performed increasingly important roles in security and the potential for waging war. Also, space travel, including putting a man on the moon, would not have been possible without the remarkable computer. World War III will be different from past wars in terms of utilizing computers, cameras, and satellites. An article in *The Electronic System Design Magazine* explains what war will be like in an age of computers "Today's war machines think," the article proclaims, the article is entitled, "Artificial Intelligence and Armageddon."

> The joke that the IQ of weapons exceeds the IQ of the individuals using them is no longer a joke. In the 1970s, signalmen began outnumbering infantry in the army. Similar parallels exist for other branches of the

military. Now, computers increasingly govern the military, supplanting—rather than supplementing—judgments of commanders and soldiers. A computer-in-chief threatens to usurp the commander-in-chief.

Still, the "Formal Rules" of artificial intelligence cannot represent (or replace) common sense or intuition. Raw computer output is never unequivocal. Although artificial intelligence should be heeded when appropriate, it is unconstitutional to delegate to machines the power to initiate and wage war.

In 1983, the Defense Advanced Research Projects Agency (DARPA) proposed a strategic computing initiative. Projects underway include an automatic naval battle management system, an autonomous fighter pilot, and an autonomous tank. Autonomous weapons are preconfigured to execute belligerent acts according to digitally evaluated conditions. They initiate hostilities and select targets, and so generate, rather than comply with, military orders. This is a chilling abdication of military responsibilities, especially in the execution of rules of engagement, where the exercise of human discretion is traditionally enjoined. The much reported strategic defense initiative (SDI) is a prime example. SDI depends upon knocking out hostile missiles in their boost phase, while still over foreign territory, and so requires an entirely automatic response to sensor detections. Software and artificial intelligence are to have a pivotal role in SDI. The president's orders will be preprogrammed.

The growing trend toward strategic computerization is crowned by the Rand

Strategy Assessment System (RSAS). The purpose of RSAS is to compute decisions by rationally weighing the probability and value of each possible outcome. A central program module is named "Blue Agent" manifestations of which are stored on line as "Sam 1" and "Sam 2" etc. Each Sam includes a set of attributes prescribing "Temperament." An example temperament attribute is "Risk Proclivity," which is represented on a scale of one to three.

RSAS is not just another war game. Networked through the joint analysis directorate in the Pentagon, RSAS applications provide the national command authorities (NCA) with the decision-making guidance during crises. Launch on warning, nuclear first use, and other escalatory decisions are modeled by RSAS.

The Pentagon swears that only the president can launch on warning, and that he might: but the de facto truth is that only A-I can launch on warning, and that it might. A critical look at the presently evolving system shows that after sensors register the flight of missiles, we become wholly dependent on computers to recognize the statistical pattern and estimate the probability of attack, while in turn scheduling these judgments quickly enough to advise and execute a responsive launch of minuteman and MX missiles prior to a predefined "use them or lose them" deadline.

The next articles to which I refer appeared in March 1988 *Bible in the News* magazine, page sixteen. These revealing items demonstrate the potential for robots already in existence and also the violent capabilities for such machines when they go out of control:

It's almost frightening. These creatures walk, talk, react to both discomfort and pleasure, and can put in a day's work. The age of the "intelligent" machine is upon us, and nowhere is that more clearly demonstrated than at the Franklin Institute's major exhibit called "Robots and Beyond: The age of the intelligent machine." It's sci-fi up close as visitors encounter robots that can read from a printed page, can weigh and mix chemicals . . . can compose-and perform-original music . . . The word robot comes from a Czech word meaning "Serf," and even a century ago, the French had a robotic device that controlled a loom. But the robotic revolution really began in the 1940s when George Devol unleashed on the world a multi-purpose robot that could control machines. By 1959, the planet corporation had refined the "Creature" for commercial use. So the Franklin Institute is out to show us that the brave new world is not some futuristic fable. Not with robots expected to perform household chores (They do windows) . . . It also raises all sorts of questions about our co-existence, as humans, with these brilliant babies of technology . . . (The exhibit) will leave you convinced that artificial intelligence is ready to revolutionize the world, whether or not you're ready . . . The exhibit will probably leave you with the sense that in their best . . . application, robots can enhance human life and elevate it from drudgery. (*Burlington County Times* [July 10, 1987])

Bible in the News continues,

consider this warning: Japanese authorities are investigating a series of mysterious deaths in which industrial robots suddenly attacked and killed humans. Ten people have been killed by robots in the last eight years, officials say. And while some were linked to operating errors, in some cases the robots suddenly started working for unexplained reasons. While a life of ease has its attractions, it also has it liabilities. ("Future Shock," *Newsday* [May 29, 1987]) I Thessalonians 5:3 warns: "For when they shall say, peace and safety: then sudden destruction cometh upon them . . . And they shall not escape." Perhaps some sort of computerized robotic system will be key to the reign of antichrist and the False Prophet of Revelation. Revelation 13:14-15 foretells that dreadful day: "And (The False Prophet) deceiveth them that dwell on the earth by the means of those miracles which he had power to do in the sight of the beast: saying . . . That they should make an image to the beast . . . And he had power to give life unto the image of the beast . . . And cause that as many as would not worship the image of the beast should be killed." Robotics may be key to the future in more ways than one.

We need to also consider a large robot army under the electronic control of Antichrist. A killing machine, basically impregnable and not subject to human-type injuries, is a formidable force indeed. Consider Joel's description of a fierce army which could very well be a body of mechanized warriors:

A day of darkness and of gloominess, a day of clouds and of thick darkness, as the morning spread upon the mountains: a great people and a strong: There hath not been ever the like, neither shall be anymore after it, even to the years of many generations. A fire devoureth before them; and behind them a flame burneth: The land is as the

Garden of Eden before them, and behind them a desolate wilderness: Yea, and nothing shall escape them. The appearance of them is as the appearance of horses: And as horsemen, so shall they run. Like the noise of chariots on the tops of mountains shall they leap, like the noise of a flame of fire that devoureth the stubble, as a strong people set in battle array. Before their face the people shall be much pained: All faces shall gather blackness. They shall run like mighty men: They shall climb the wall like men of war: and they shall march every one on his ways, and they shall not break their ranks: neither shall one thrust another: they shall walk every one in his path: and when they fall upon the sword, they shall not be wounded. They shall climb up upon the houses: They shall enter in at the windows like a thief. The earth shall quake before them: The heavens shall tremble, the sun and the moon shall be dark, and the stars shall withdraw their shining. (Joel 2:2-10)

The achievements of scientists using computers and artificial intelligence are truly mind boggling as they utilize their expensive toys to look into the future or backwards into the past. In an article, written in March of 1988, entitled "Fast and Smart—Designers Race to Build the Supercomputers of the Future," *Time* discusses some of these expensive toys. There are as many as three hundred

supercomputers now working at tasks as diverse as ferreting out oil deposits, analyzing muscle structures and creating special effects for Hollywood films. With the spread of supercomputer networks, high-speed computing power is available to anyone with a personal computer and a telephone hookup. "The world will never be the same." Says Doyle Knight, Director of the John Von

Newumann National Computer Center in
Princeton, NJ. "Soon every industry, every
science, every walk of life will in some way
be touched by supercomputing.

Supercomputers are giving scientists unprecedented access to hidden worlds both large and small. Using the prodigious power of the Cray at the San Diego Supercomputer Center, researchers Mark Ellisman and Stephen Young are studying a pair of noodle-like structures in the brains of alzheimer's victims that scientists think may be a cause of premature dementia.

Northwestern University professor Arthur Freeman used a Cray-2 to produce a stunning portrait of the atomic structure of a new superconductor that carries an electric current freely at 283 degrees fahrenheit. The Cray X-MP at the University of Illinois has produced a dazzling array of colorful animations, from the rolling birth of a tornado to the supersonic fountains that spew forth from black holes at the centers of galaxies.

Says Nobel physicist Kenneth Wilson of Cornell University: "An astronomer with a telescope can observe the universe over a period of 50 years. But an astrophysicist with a supercomputer can "see" billions of years into the past and future."

Concerning artificial intelligence, a highly controversial area of scientific research, the next article is sinister and frightening to say the least, and definitely relates to George Orwell's world and the beast kingdom of Revelation. In a November 1987 issue of OMNI on page twenty-four, an interesting article appeared entitled "When Robots Rule the World." OMNI reports that Carl Hewitt, an associate professor of electrical engineering and computer science at MIT, believes that computers will help us "sidestep" nuclear catastrophe.

Carl Hewitt scares the h — out of me, but
perhaps he is right: use intelligent
computers to help govern us and robotic
police to help keep us in line. Hewitt sees the

future of humanity in the quickly developing field of parallel computers, the massively powerful machines that will process information in a fashion similar to the human brain's. Hewitt also believes that the coming of such high-powered marvels will allow the human race to sidestep the threat of nuclear war by equally sharing control with machines.

In fact, he is already at work designing ways of making computer systems more reliable, a step that will lay the foundation for such sharing. Hewitt's idea is to make computers more like the U. S. Congress—that is, give them the capability to not only process a vast amount of knowledge but also evaluate and debate it before coming to a decision about what to do. Eventually such a sophisticated electronic organization would be capable of analyzing world conflicts and choosing appropriate actions. It would do so in a way, says Hewitt, that's "not left to human whim and emotion, with nationalistic states threatening each other."

Of course, Hewitt's solution depends on whether countries would be willing to share power with computers and be policed by robots. One can already see the bumper stickers: When Guns are Outlawed, Only Robots Will Have Guns! Governments will undoubtedly balk when it comes to handing over control. But Hewitt thinks the resistance will ebb under certain circumstances. "People could become very scared and very threatened," he explains, "By small nuclear wars popping off here and there—like between India and Pakistan or between Israel and the Arabs."

George Williams, a professor emeritus of

Divinity at Harvard, believes Hewitt may be right in his assessment of the situation. "In the back of my thoughts about computers taking over is my fear that we are not capable—as human beings—of taking care of ourselves." Williams explains. "We are just going mad. I don't think we can remain humane very much longer. I think computers could take the rattle out of life. I just don't see how we can keep going on the way we are."

But then there's another chilling factor to consider. Could we lose control over the system we create to protect us?

In a lighter vein, consider an experimental computer with the knowledge of a six year old child and still growing in its fund of artificial intelligence. This fascinating item appeared in *OMNI* in June 1988. The headlines on page forty-five read, "Brain Trusts":

Four years old, it's full of promise, possessing the potential for deep intelligence. It knows who Napoleon Bonaparte was, can describe the port city of Algiers, and will tell you how many wheels a car has. If it continues to learn at its present rate, if it doesn't encounter some insurmountable barrier, it will be as "smart" as a six-year-old child. Or so it's creator, thirty-eight year old Doug Lenat, believes. The former professor of artificial intelligence (AL) at both Stanford and Carnegie-Mellon University has developed CYC (pronounced psych) and short for cyclopedia), one of the most daring projects in AL today. In fact, if a poll were taken of AL researchers, it might well be voted the project least likely to succeed. Lenat's goal, you see, is to create a computer that has all the general knowledge—or as AL researchers call it, common sense—of a child, a computer that can think for itself and learn new knowledge as humans do. Then, says Lenat, the door will be open for such futuristic items as an intelligent wristwatch that would serve as a sort of traveling companion to advise and comfort its owner.

Lenat has long been known as one of the gutsier and more outspoken wizards of AL, a man who's not afraid to take on the impossible or to criticize his colleagues for their timidity. As he puts it, "Most AL people are spending their research lives creating bumps on logs."

Although he won accolades early in his career for work in machine learning, CYC is by far his most adventurous effort. Lenat himself gives the project only a 50 percent chance of success and warns that he won't know until the end of the project (about six years from now) whether it will work.

If it does, however, the payoff will change the field of artificial intelligence forever. "It's the most exciting thing on the horizon" says artificial intelligence Guru Marvin Minsky. "I think it's the best hope for making machines do things that people would call smart."

If you can envision a robot playing chess or delivering meals on wheels, then you know how fast robots are coming into the market place. A technology article in *Newsweek* 28 March 1988 says, "Robots Find Their Place"—They aren't quite ready yet to replace humans, but their usefulness is growing:

There are robots in your future—and these aren't figments of George Lucas's imagination. Already in the United States more than 30,000 robots perform a remarkable variety of tasks, everything from assembling computers, artillery shells and vacuum cleaners to popping frozen cutlets into TV-dinner trays. Robots have assisted with brain surgery in California, cancer research in Maryland and cleanup at the Three Mile Island nuclear plant. Experimental robots drive vans, harvest oranges and care for the disabled. And researchers are now producing a new generation of commercial automatons that, within a decade, could make working robots an every day sight in offices and shopping malls.

Robots still can't match the exuberant promises of the early '80s, when boosters predicted that R2-D2 would soon be vacuuming our floors and washing the dishes. "Our anthem was "We shall overclaim," says one researcher. But in the new era of lowered expectations, technology has become more practical and somewhat less expensive. Five years ago a welding robot cost $150,000: now it costs just half. A new robot arm from adept technology is programmed simply by choosing items from a menu: a human worker can teach the robot's eyes to recognize a new part in less than 10 minutes. And Detroit robotmaker GMF Robotics has developed a computer program that automatically plans the robots needed to assemble a new product even as an engineer is designing the product itself.

In keeping with this enlightening article, "McRobot," shows us the latest developments in the fast-food field. Quoting OMNI, June 1988, page thirty-seven:

A robotic hamburger maker, guided by computer and cued by photo-optic cells, could be the answer to the woes of the fast-food industry—now mired in a growth slump and faced with manpower shortages.

True, the prototype designed by translab, a Menomonie, Wisconsin, research-and-development firm; still can't handle such tricky haute cuisine options as lettuce, tomatoes, or onions. But give it time, says translab president David L. Brenholt, whose company built the $20,000 robot for a food-lab cafeteria run by the home economics department at the University of Wisconsin's stout campus.

A series of conveyer belts bounces patties and the crowns and heels of the buns, as they call their tops and bottoms in the burger business, through a cooking tunnel, five sets at a time. At journey's end, less than two minutes later, the meat and buns reach photooptic sensors that determine if the orders have been properly cooked. Then, if all goes well, the robot arm flips over the browned buns, plops the patties inside, and presto, the finished product emerges on a final conveyer.

Says Craig W. Schowalter, a University of Wisconsin fast-food-operation instructor "We're on the cutting edge of hamburger technology with some chain-speed adjustments. This robot's second generation could handle ten hamburgers a minute.

The year of the robot could also bring us very close to a Babel-like world. A recent article in a Canadian newspaper *The Globe and Mail*, September 18, 1987, describes how language can be instantly unscrambled or translated into a number of different languages:

Polylingual program unscrambles Babel— People unable to speak a word of each other's language may soon be able to talk to each other by phone—and understand each other. Prototype equipment has been developed by British telecom PLC over the past three years that can translate English into several languages using the "World's first system of instantaneous speech translation by computer." The system will be demonstrated by the British phone company at an . . . exhibition in Geneva . . . the equipment translates English into French, German, Spanish, Swedish, and Italian, and the reverse capability is being developed. This will then also make possible translation between any pair of these languages, such as French-German or Swedish-Italian. Each speaker has a microphone linked to a personal computer. The computers are linked by phone line capable of handling data. The user speaks into his mike and the computer repeats the sentence in its own synthetic voice to check that the words have been correctly understood. Then the originating computer sends the message to the distant computer, which translates the words and "Speaks" them out in the other language . . . The system is based on a set of 400 common business phrases that are stored in each user's computer memory . . . The computers are programmed to recognize only 100 key words . . . These are used to identify the appropriate phrases, reducing the word recognition task involved. The system also recognizes spoken proper names . . . and makes no attempt to translate them . . . The names are repeated in the original speaker's voice."

It is evident that the computer has vastly changed our present world, and the robot with a fifth generation computer for a brain, will create a regimented type of society dominated by data banks and internetworking telecommunications. Quoting a revolutionary type of article in *Discover Magazine*, December 1987:

> Worked hard at the office today, didn't you, sure, but it says here that you also made three personal phone calls, spent two hours away from your computer terminal, and when you were working, made six unnecessary keystrokes and 17 typos.

> Welcome to the age of the electronic supervisor. A new study by the Federal Office of Technology Assessment reveals that the days of the ... office manager may be coming to an end: running the show instead in more and more offices is the see-all, tell-all computer.

> The study, commissioned by Congressman Don Edwards of California, indicates that as many as 6 million workers nationwide are now scrutinized by computers for all or part of their workday. Those whose jobs involve desktop terminals are the most vulnerable . . . bank tellers, mailroom employees, and other away-from-the desk workers are at risk too . . .

> New technology has also led to absolutely silent telephone monitoring that permits (eavesdropping) on telephone solicitors and operators. Before long . . . professional and managerial workers may be monitored as well. The report addresses a number of troubling issues raised by all this . . . most important, the questions of whether electronic monitoring is an invasion of employee privacy. "Of all the things we don't want, the last is a surveillance society," says Edwards. "But it appears we're headed in that direction."

"The problem is distressingly large"
Edwards said. "At the moment it appears to
be out of control."

Be advised, the computer-camera-robot monitored
society will not be out of control. When the standing image
in the form of a metallic man of Daniel chapter 2 comes alive
in Revelation chapter 13, the whole world will be controlled
by the Antichrist and his image. . . . "And he had power to
give life unto the image of the beast, that the image of the
beast should both speak, and cause that as many as would
not worship the image of the beast should be killed" (Rev.
13:15).

This will be a fearful time upon the earth without any
historic parallel. But—praise God—the Lord Jesus Christ
will return from Heaven at the end of the Tribulation to
smash this terrible image of the beast: Cast alive the Antichrist and false prophet into the lake of fire. And the saints
of God will inherit the kingdom. "But the saints of the most
high shall take the kingdom, and possess the kingdom for
ever, even for ever and ever" (Dan. 7:18).

Nine

IN MAN'S IMAGE

Man's image experienced a drastic change after Adam's sin. In the beginning, Adam had a God-like aura or image until he disobeyed God and lost this holy covering. We read about man's altered image in the book of Genesis:

> This is the book of the generations of Adam. In the day that God created man, in the likeness of God made he him; Male and female created he them; and blessed them, and called their name Adam, in the day when they were created. And Adam lived an hundred and thirty years, and begat a son in his own likeness, after his image; and called his name Seth. (Gen. 5:1-2)

Today, we witness man's ultimate and greatest achievements in promoting his own image in the cosmos. Politicians and preachers regard their public image as all important. So do movie and television stars of every kind. The image is the key to success; it must be carefully cultivated and protected at any cost.

People are not only concerned about the image they project: but they devote many waking hours viewing or studying images on all kinds of screens, for example, television, computer, and movie screens. Man's pre-occupation with imagery is at an all-time high, even reaching out into the heavens by satellites and bouncing back these sundry and diverse images to any selected point on the face of the earth.

The scientific accomplishments of twentieth century man in complex fields of imaging, confirm God's indictment against sinful man, born of Adam's race, in perverting God's image before the world. The book of Romans says, "Because that, when they knew God, they glorified Him not as God, neither were thankful; but became vain in their imaginations, and their foolish heart was darkened. Professing themselves to be wise, they became fools, And changed the glory of the incorruptible God into an image made like to corruptible man, and to birds, and four-footed beasts, and creeping things" (Rom. 1:21-23).

This once more causes us to examine the greatest abomination in God's sight which will happen in the closing days of man's dispensation. I refer of course to the image of the beast that comes alive and will ultimately control the activities of the world. In the book of Revelation, John says:

> And deceiveth them that dwell on the earth by the means of those miracles which he had power to do in the sight of the beast; saying to them that dwell on the earth, that they should make an image to the beast, which had the wound by a sword, and did live. And he had power to give life unto the image of the beast, that the image of the beast should both speak, and cause that as many as would not worship the image of the beast should be killed. And he causeth all, both small and great, rich and poor, free and bond, to receive a mark in their right hand, or in their foreheads: And that no man might buy or sell, save he that had the mark, or the name of the beast, or the number of his name. (Rev. 13:14-17)

Again, I suggest that this fearful image is the one revealed by God in a dream to Nebuchadnezzar—the first empire builder of the Gentiles—and subsequently interpreted by Daniel:

> Thou, O King, sawest, and behold a great image. This great image, whose brightness was excellent, stood before thee; and the form thereof was terrible. This image's head was of fine gold, his breast and his arms of silver, his belly and his thighs of brass, His legs of iron, his feet part of iron and part of clay. Thou sawest till that a stone was cut out without hands, which smote the image upon his feet that were of iron and clay, and break them to pieces.

> Then was the iron, the clay, the brass, the silver, and the gold, broken to pieces together, and became like the chaff of the summer threshing floors; and the wind carried them away, that no place was found for them: and the stone that smote the image became a great mountain, and filled the whole earth.

> This is the dream; and we will tell the interpretation thereof before the king. Thou, O king, art a king of kings: for the God of heaven hath given thee a kingdom, power, and strength, and glory. And wheresoever the children of men dwell, the beasts of the field and the fowls of the heaven hath he given into thine hand, and hath made thee ruler over them all. Thou art this head of gold.

> And after thee shall arise another kingdom inferior to thee, and another third kingdom of brass, which shall bear rule over all the earth. And the fourth kingdom shall be strong as iron: for as much, as iron breaketh in pieces and subdueth all things: and as iron

that breaketh all these, shall it break in pieces and bruise.

And whereas thou sawest the feet and toes, part of potters' clay, and part of iron, the kingdom shall be divided; but there shall be in it of the strength of the iron, for as much as thou sawest the iron mixed with miry clay. And as the toes of the feet were part of iron, and part of clay, so the kingdom shall be partly strong, and partly broken. And whereas thou sawest iron mixed with miry clay, they shall mingle themselves with the seed of men: but they shall not cleave one to another, even as iron is not mixed with clay.

And in the days of these kings shall the God of heaven set up a kingdom, which shall never be destroyed: and the kingdom shall not be left to other people, but is shall break in pieces and consume all these kingdoms, and it shall stand for ever. For as much as thou sawest that the stone was cut out of the mountain without hands, and that it break in pieces the iron, the brass, the clay, the silver, and the gold; the great God hath made known to the king what shall come to pass hereafter; and the dream is certain, and the interpretation thereof sure.

In chapter 2 of this book, I have already suggested that this metallic man-like image of Daniel chapter 2 will come alive in fulfillment of the book of Revelation 13:14,15. By means of fantastic technology, this electronic image (probably a giant robot with a fifth generation computer for a brain), a kind of bionic man, will be able to observe and utterly dominate all the people on this planet.

Such a fantasy world will be tied together by fiber-optics, under twenty-four hour surveillance by satellites, cameras, and cables, and orders will go forth by international and interstellar television in three dimensional transmission to every village, island and continent.

That such a bizarre scenario is virtually already within man's grasp is aptly demonstrated by a news article that appeared in *The Daily Oklahoman*, September 20, 1988. "Humanlike Computers Moving to Real World":

> The science-fiction fantasy of a computer that works like a living brain is beginning to emerge as a reality, with applications, major government funding, market research and two publicly traded companies attesting to the validity of the concept.
>
> Such computers are based on a technology called neural networks because they are patterned after the interconnected nerve cells, or neurons, in the brain.
>
> "We are trying to build a brain and we are trying to build it out of brainlike parts," said Bernard Widrow, a professor at Stanford University and a pioneer in the neural network field.
>
> "It might take a thousand years to build a whole brain," he cautioned. But he added that "in the next decade some useful applications will result."
>
> In fact, although most neural network applications are still in the developmental stage, at least four are currently being used. The most sophisticated is a system that evaluates mortgage loans and determines whether they should be approved.
>
> "Overall (the system) is found to be much more consistent in its classifications . . . than are human underwriters," according to Nestor Inc, the application's developer.
>
> Neural networks are a type of artificial intelligence. The most common artificial

intelligence approach, expert systems, are programmed with a set of rules and make determinations by applying those rules.

But the system breaks down when a situation occurs for which there is no prelearned rule, the kinds of situations living brains encounter all the time.

A brain's billions of nerve cells are all interconnected and change with experience. With all the nerve cells working on the same problem together, even a slug can perform a simple task, like recognizing an object instantly, that would require a standard computer to go through millions of calculations.

Neural networks try to simulate those interconnections electronically so that they can learn by experience instead of being programmed. Researchers say their greatest potential at this point is object recognition. Applications have been developed to verify check signatures and identify heart disease by reading electrocardiograms.

Life as we know it today is already dominated by the resident computer, and various and sundry data banks. As one scientist verbalized: in our modern computer world, we have already passed the point of no return. Traffic and commerce, including the big board on Wall Street, would all cease to function if our multiple computers should simultaneously malfunction.

Already, people are nearly as dependent on internetworking computer systems as the regimented world society described in the book of Revelation (the society of the Antichrist). We are even comfortable using the numbers and marks of the universal product code in preparation for the coming time of the Great Tribulation (See Rev. 13:16, 17).

Young people today probably wonder if there was really life before the computer. Life for many people under thirty-five is becoming influenced by the rational computer scene dominated by the image. By using the telephone and the computer screen, people can do their shopping, pay their monthly bills and prepare their income tax return.

Teen-agers can become so preoccupied with electronic fantasies, that they seemingly move into the stereotyped world of computers and temporarily forget the real world. Such an example appeared in *Reader's Digest*, October 1988, page forty-seven under the heading "Computer Syndrome":

> Warning to computer freaks: excessive preoccupation with your machine can reveal a dormant psychosis, report doctors in Denmark's *Weekly Journal For Doctors*.
>
> One Danish 18-year-old was so absorbed that he neglected his friends and spent 12-16 hours a day at his home computer. "He merged with it," say psychiatrists Eva Jensen and Erik Simonsen and psychologist Bent Brok. He began to think in computer-programming language, suffered from insomnia and anxiety and finally was unable to distinguish between his programs and the real world. He had to be hospitalized and treated for psychotic illness.
>
> The computer trade itself recognizes the problem. Lars Knudsen, director of a high-technology information agency, estimates there are 5000 computer freaks in Denmark. Typically, they are between ages 12 and 18 and 95 percent of them are boys. They sleep into the afternoon and then sit in front of the screen until four in the morning. As their preoccupation grows, the always rational computer becomes a substitute for human contact.

Our computer-dependent society may also come to dread a computer virus more than a human virus. Such an infection could shut down huge systems at the cost of millions of dollars. For example, at the *Providence Journal Bulletin* newspaper, one of the financial reporters sat down to write a story and as usual put a floppy disk into one of the newspaper's computers.

She heard a high pitched squeal, and on the screen flashed the words: disk error. She took the disk to the paper's computer detective, and buried on the disk, he found a virus and the words: welcome to the dungeon . . . contact us for vaccination.

Over the next six months, Scheidler, the systems engineer at the paper, checked out fifteen hundred to two thousand floppy disks. He found 150–200 were infected by the virus. To this day, he doesn't know how.

Also, Donald Burleson was recently prosecuted by the district attorney's office in Fort Worth, Texas for planting a computer virus that wiped out 168,000 payroll records from U.S. P.A. and I.R.A. company computers.

John McAfee—President of Interpath Corp of Santa Clara California—was recently interviewed by *U.S.A. Today* on the subject, "Computer Infections are Invisible, Deadly" (September 22, 1988, page 7A):

> How much of a threat are computer viruses that change or destroy a computer's information bank, and how many companies have been hit so far?

McAfee: The threat is increasing. We have records of 300,000 computer infections to date, with a fairly even mix between industry, government and academic. The threat is greater for individuals and organizations that use the public-domain or share software.

USA Today: Is there any reason to be concerned that a computer virus could shut down the phone system or infiltrate our bank machines, even a military computer?

McAfee: The security measures that currently exist within organizations like banks, the phone company or the military are geared toward threats from individuals, not from viruses. Viruses are spread usually by friendly hands, people who work within the facility itself. And the people who spread the virus usually do not know what they are doing. The virus is invisible and cannot be detected except through the use of specialized tools. So there is indeed a risk of a major problem within a secure organization.

USA Today: How does a virus make its way into a computer?

McAfee: The virus is originally developed by the perpetrator and spread primarily through the public-domain channels—bulletin boards, or distribution of public-domain software. From there, it is spread by anyone who comes in contact with any infected system, so that an employee of a corporation may have a computer at home that becomes infected through a child's use of the system that may have received the virus from school. The employee then may use the system at home, transfer disks to the work environment, and thereby infect the entire organization.

USA Today: What has been the most serious computer virus attack so far?

McAfee: Probably the IBM Christmas attack last year. The IBM worldwide data network is composed of nearly 350,000 terminals. That entire network was shut down for a number of hours due to a virus attack. The cost of lost time has totaled over $11 million in that single attack. I anticipate that within 18 months, attacks that reach that magnitude will be commonplace.

USA Today: What can computer users do to protect themselves from being hit by a virus, and if you are hit by one, how hard is it to get rid of?

McAfee: Avoid the use of public-domain software. Don't share data and programs with friends or co-workers, limit the transfer of data between personal computers, and never use software when you are unsure of the origin.

USA Today: Where did the computer virus come from?

McAfee: The first computer virus was developed at the Xerox Corp in 1973 by a couple of systems engineers as an experiment. Nothing much transpired in the virus world until 1981–82, when academicians began to write papers about the potential of computer viruses. The first public-domain virus that actually infected the world on a large scale was written by two brothers in Pakistan in 1986. That virus has now spread around the world and is the single most infectious virus around.

It appears that everything made after the image of man is eventually tarnished and polluted. The computer, twentieth century man's toy, has become the innovative catalyst for big business in this information age. However, the computer and the robot will most likely become the Frankenstein of the Antichrist's commercial monopoly which compels all the world to work, buy, and sell—using his mark and his number.

"And he causeth all, both small and great, rich and poor, free and bond, to receive a mark in their right hand, or in their foreheads: And that no man might buy or sell, save he that had the mark, or the name of the beast, or the number of his name" (Rev. 13:16, 17).

Ten

THE REVIVED ROMAN EMPIRE IMAGE

There is no greater prophetic truth in the Bible than the certainty of the revival of the Roman Empire at the end of the age. Rome was in power when the Lord Jesus Christ came the first time, and Rome will again be in power when He returns. For centuries, even as Europe stood hopelessly divided and embroiled in seemingly endless wars, students of prophecy have stood firm in their conviction that ten nations, which were once within the geographic, political, and religious boundaries of Rome, would again form a federation of states. This federation would, in the last days, produce a world dictator.

It is of major importance that the Common Market came into being on March 25, 1957 at the invitation of Rome, and the first meeting was held in the Vatican itself. Six of the present Common Market member nations attended that first historic meeting. Dr. J. A. Seiss, in 1860, made the following observation concerning the rebirth of Rome in his commentary on Revelation: "Think for a moment, for there is such power that is everywhere clamoring for a common code, a common currency, common weights and measures: and which is not likely to be silenced or to stop till it has secured a common center of its own independent basis, whence to dictate to all countries and to exercise its own peculiar rule on all the kings and nations of the earth . . . which Western Europe in its own defense will presently be compelled to construct . . ."

Although Dr. Seiss made this prophetic observation 130 years ago, it is as current as our morning newspaper. Here, I quote from page ten of the January/February edition of *Europe,* the official publication of the Common Market Alliance:

> Ever since World War II, statesmen and commentators on both sides of the Atlantic have wrestled with the dilemma of Europe's defense dependence on the United States. As long ago as 1962, President John F. Kennedy encapsulated what he saw as the solution to the dilemma, when he called for a stronger European "pillar" in the Atlantic Alliance. Yet, while many echoed his aspiration, nothing changed on the ground . . . A certain degree of European weakness . . . ensured the American presence and American leadership of the Alliance. The American presence in Europe provided Russia with a guarantee against German revanchism, and legitimized the presence of the Soviet forces in Eastern Europe. The dilemma was not entirely comfortable, but it seemed frozen solid. . . . To an unprecedented degree, Americans are now aware that the North Atlantic Treaty Organizational (NATO) weakness in conventional defense, and its dependence on nuclear weapons, pose terrible potential danger for the guaranteeing super power . . . The problem, as the Germans are fond of repeating, is not that the Americans are too strong, but that the Europeans are too weak.

The Common Market is also rapidly developing its own space program. Quoting again from page twenty-two of the 1985 January/February edition of *Europe:*

> There must be few rags-to-riches fairy tales to match the story of Europe's efforts   to

become a major rival to the United States and
the Soviet Union in the field of space technology and, in particular, to develop its own
ariane satellite-launching rocket . . . *Ariane*
has enjoyed a record of 100 percent success.
The three remaining launches in the promo-
tional series have been followed by three
fully commercial launches . . . All have taken
place from ESA's launch site at Kourou in
French Guiana. Any technical concerns that
Europe might not have been able to meet the
U.S. challenge seem to have been finally put
to rest . . . Having successfully fulfilled the
task that they set themselves 10 years ago,
the member countries of ESA are now looking toward the future. In particular, they are
discussing eventual collaboration on an
entirely new type of *Ariane*, which would
become available by the end of 1990s,
capable not merely of putting satellites into
orbit, but also manned space vehicles and
thus perhaps servicing a European space
station.

The conclusion presented in this article on advancing
European space technology is that the Common Market will
be able to challenge both the United States and Russia in the
"Star Wars" race within the next decade.

Over twenty-five hundred years ago, the prophet
Daniel foretold the parade of empires, which would march
upon the world scene from Babylon until the time the
Messiah would come and establish an everlasting kingdom.
The fourth empire from Babylon was clearly defined as
Rome by the prophet:

And the Fourth Kingdom shall be strong as
iron: forasmuch, as iron breaketh in pieces
and subdueth all things: and as iron that
breaketh all these, shall it break in pieces and
bruise. And whereas thou sawest the feet
and toes, part of potter's clay, and part of

iron, the kingdom shall be divided: but
there shall be in it of the strength of the iron,
forasmuch as thou sawest the   iron mixed
with miry clay. And as the toes of the feet
were part of iron, and part of clay, so the
kingdom shall be partly strong, and partly
broken . . . And in the days of these kings
shall the God of Heaven set up a kingdom,
which shall never be destroyed: And the
kingdom shall not be left to other people, but
it shall break in pieces and consume all these
kingdoms, and it shall stand for ever." (Dan.
2:40-44)

The Word of God relating to the future of nations reveals
that the Roman Empire would be broken into pieces, but
when ten of the pieces which broke off formed an alliance
at the end of the age, and the Roman Empire was pieced
back together, then the world would know that the coming
of the Messiah (to establish his own kingdom on earth) was
near.

Daniel prophesied that as the coming of the Messiah
drew near, the iron chunks would be broken up into much
smaller pieces. It is a fact of modern history that after World
War II, the European colonial system began to break up, just
as Daniel prophesied. The June 1975 edition of *Reader's
Digest* in an article entitled "The United States and the New
Society" made the following observations:

The United States and the new Society is
nothing new to Americans . . . But there is
something new in international pronouncements . . . It is almost as if American opinion
now acknowledged that there was no escap-
ing involvement in the emergent world
society. What happened in the early 1970s is
that for the first time the world felt the
impact of what I shall call the British
Revolution which began in 1947 with the
granting by socialist Britain of independence

to socialist India. In slow, then rapid order, the great empires of the world—with the major exception of the former Czarist empire—broke up into independent states: The original U.N. membership of 51 grew to 138 . . . Socialist doctrine as it developed in Britain was anti-American. More anti-American, surely, than it ever was anti-Soviet . . . In the first half of the 20th Century, British Civil servants took the doctrine of British socialism to the colonies, a domain which covered one quarter of the earth's surface. By 1950 not communists but Fabian Socialists could claim that the largest portion of the world's population lived in regimes of their fashioning . . .

In 1957, six of the colonial powers that belonged to the Roman Empire joined together in a trade agreement called the European Economic Community, or Common Market. However, when the headquarters for the Common Market was erected in Brussels, Belgium, ten flagpoles were placed in front. This was in accordance with Bible prophecy.

The six charter members were Belgium, France, the Netherlands, Italy, Luxembourg, and West Germany. The alliance was confined to six members until 1973, when Henry Kissinger persuaded the Common Market members to fill the remaining four flagpoles in front of the capitol building, and so Norway, England, Denmark, and Ireland were proposed for membership. This would have completed the ten-nation alliance. However, Norway withdrew and Greece, on January 1, 1981, became the tenth member.

As we look to the Common Market of Europe today, we see it emerging as a solid union of states. The differences within these ten nations (that have kept them divided and at war with each other since the break up of the Roman Empire fifteen hundred years ago) are being reconciled through a single parliament and a common president of the union. It is evident that had there been a unified Europe, it could have conquered and controlled the world. If Napoleon had a unified federation of European nations, he could have easily conquered the world; and the same could be said of Kaiser Wilhelm and Adolph Hitler.

The November 1980 edition of *Moody Monthly* made the following observation on the Common Market of Europe:

> The Bible does not specifically name the nations in the Western confederacy, but many Bible scholars agree that the image of Nebuchadnezzar's dream (Dan. 2:31-33) portrays the whole sweep of Gentile world history . . . The image's feet and toes . . . foretell a reappearance or continuation of the great power of Rome. The toes make it clear that ten kingdoms will form this final Gentile power (Dan. 2:41, 42).

> The number ten is also mentioned in Daniel 7:7, 24 and Revelation 17:12. Until recent times, no such ten-nation empire existed . . . Will the market stop at ten? There is talk that both Spain and Portugal could join. But there is also opposition . . . Daniel saw that the Western confederacy will be strong as iron (Dan. 2:40). In fact, it is to become a world superpower. The fourth beast shall be the fourth kingdom upon earth, which shall be diverse from all kingdoms, and shall devour the whole earth, and shall tread it down, and break it in pieces (Dan. 7:23). No successor to the Roman Empire has ever achieved this kind of power.

> For centuries, the continental neighbors of Europe have quarreled. Twice in this century, their nationalism has flamed into global warfare. Now, all has changed. The Common Market may easily become the most powerful economic, political, and military union on earth. Is it merely coin-

cidence that a long-fragmented continent,
separated by different languages, cultures,
histories, and traditions should form a new
federation . . . ?

Already the member nations form the world's largest
trading bloc. Their gross national product is growing. Their
population is huge. They have negotiated commercial or
association agreements with more than ninety countries.
They have special trade and aid relationships with more
than fifty former colonies of Africa, the Caribbean, and the
Pacific. All this before the addition of Greece.

Henry Kissinger of the Security Council of the United
States said that in the future

we could be confronted by an expanded
Europe comprising a Common Market of at
least ten full members, associated member-
ships for the EFTA (European free trade
area) neutrals, and preferential trade
agreements with at least the Mediterranean
and most of Africa. This block will account
for about half of world trade, compared with
our   15   percent: It will hold monetary
reserves approaching twice our own: and it
will even be able to outvote us constantly in
the international economic organizations."

State religion was, from the beginning, an integral part
of the Roman Empire. Rome built the Pantheon as a place
for all the gods of the empire. Religion and government
became a theocracy through the god who was over all,
Caesar. After A.D. 325, Constantine made Christianity the
state religion, and it was from this system that the Catholic
church came into being. Jean Monnet recognized that if
Europe was to be reunified in the fashion of the old Roman
Empire, religious controversies must be settled, one that
would sustain the spirit of the "New Rome." The European
magazine *Realities* reported as follows: "Even more than
industrial and banking circles, the Catholic circle of the six
countries (the original six) are prepared to unite their ac-

tivities on the European scale, for they are backed by the universal church. It should be noted too that the church was very active in bringing union of the six common market countries, about two-thirds of their population is Catholic . . ."

The Vatican itself has become a world religious council that is lending its power and influence to the emergence of the revived Roman Empire. On page twelve of the January 23, 1984 edition of *Time* Magazine:

> No pope in modern times has taken such a direct interest in wielding diplomatic influence as John Paul II. Now that the U.S. has become the 107th nation with which it has diplomatic relations, the Vatican may move to establish ties with the world's other superpower. In spite of a general belief in the Vatican that the Soviet KGB was behind the 1981 shooting of the Holy father, relations with Moscow are surprisingly good. Josef Cardinal Glemp, Poland's Primate, plans to visit the Soviet Union in a few months. Before he leaves, Vatican sources say he will meet with John Paul to discuss ways to improve Vatican-Kremlin communications.

We have demonstrated how the Common Market is rapidly gaining strength economically, militarily and religiously. To demonstrate the growing influence and power of the European community, even the pope paid a visit to the headquarters of the Common Market in Brussels on May 20, 1985. Quoting May/June issue of *Europe* (1985), here is an article entitled, "Pope To Visit E.C. Commission":

> Pope John Paul II will make an historic first visit to the headquarters of the European Community in Brussels on May 20th. The Pope will meet with E.C. Commission President Jacques Delors, European Parliament President Pierre Pflimlin, and E.C. Council of Ministers President Giulio Andreotti, as

well as with members of the European Parliament and officials of E.C. member states.

Following the meetings, Pope John Paul II
will deliver an address on Europe to several
hundred European dignitaries. The address,
which will be televised in Europe, also will
be broadcast to the public over loudspeakers
in nearby Esplanade.

On page eleven of the same edition, there is a picture of
President Reagan addressing the Parliament of the
European Community in Strasbourg, France on May 8,
1985, the first American president to address the Parliament
of the Common Market.

To further demonstrate the growing togetherness and
cooperative power of the European Community, I quote
from *Europe*, page twenty-four May/June 1985:

The European Community is poised on the
starting line of a RACE against time. *RACE*
is in capital letters, because it's the name of
a breathtakingly ambitious, hugely expensive, plan to catapult Europe into the front
rank of telecommunications technology. If it
wins national government backing, it will
mean a $100-billion-plus project to
transform a splintered, inefficient and
old-fashioned telecommunications network
into the finest on earth.

Already, the E.C. commission has unveiled
plans for a 10-year program to introduce
integrated broadband communications
throughout the community. That's jargon
for a high-speed electronic system capable of
carrying mind-boggling quantities of
information in the form of reproduced
documents, video pictures and computer
conversations, as well as the dear old human
voice.

On page twenty-five of the January/February 1985 edition of *Europe* is a picture of a large man from the neck down to the waist. Just above the collar line are the heads of ten men, looking much like horns slightly titled backward, representing the leaders of the Ten Common Market Nations. This picture itself is one of the most amazing fulfillments of prophecy in these last days concerning the revived Roman Empire.

The book of Daniel says:

> After this I saw in the night visions, and behold a fourth beast, dreadful and terrible, and strong exceedingly: and it had great iron teeth: it devoured and break in pieces, and stamped the residue, with the feet of it: and it was diverse from all the beasts that were before it: and it had ten horns. I considered the horns, and, behold, there came up among them another little horn, before whom there were three of the first horns plucked up by the roots: and behold, in this horn were eyes like the eyes of man, and a mouth speaking great things. (Dan. 7:7,8)

In 1987, the Common Market or EEC observed its thirtieth anniversary and officially came of age—thirty being the age of maturity in the Bible. Now the Common Market is surging ahead in the space race, the technology explosion, and international efforts to keep the peace. Today, EEC leaders see Europe and the Common Market countries at the crossroads. In the March 1988 issue of *Europe*, an article entitled "Europe at the Crossroads," Hans Dietrich Clenscher writes:

> The paramount goal pursued by the Government of the Federal Republic of Germany upon assuming the presidency of the E. C. Council of Ministers and of European Political Co-operation (EPC) on January 1, 1988, is to impart fresh impetus to the Community, to promote European

unification and to make progress toward a European union on the basis of the Community's treaties and the Single European Act (SEA)

Democratic Europe is at a crossroads. It is up to the members of the E.C. alone whether it makes new resolute steps toward a European union or forfeits a promising future through stagnation and thus retrogression. In this era of fundamental changes and global challenges, there is a greater need than ever before for a united Community capable of acting and mastering the tasks of the future. The dynamic developments in East-West relations, enduring armed conflicts in various parts of the world, unsettled international financial markets, world economic imbalances, deep-rooted structural problems, high unemployment on the one hand, and rapid technological progress on the other, as well as the threats to our environment, call for common European efforts and responses.

The SEA has mapped out the way. Strengthening the Community's internal structures and ensuring that it is more capable of external action are imperative for safeguarding the future of all members of the Community and for Europe as a whole. The Federal Government will make every effort so that the Community gains new cohesion and lives up to its responsibility for peace in freedom and for economic stability in Europe and worldwide.

It's worthy of note that it was Germany that started World War I and World War II, and today a rebuilt robust Germany is leading the way to further unification for the Common Market Confederacy as the Federal Republic of

Germany assumes that presidency of the European Community Council of Ministers and of European Political Cooperation as of Jan. 1, 1988.

It's also singularly noteworthy that the Common Market Nations are working for total European unification and union on the basis of the Community's treaties and the Single European Act (S.E.A). I immediately picked up on the acronym for Single European Act—SEA because the final world ruler of the revived Roman Empire comes up out of the Sea, according to the book of Revelation.

> And I stood upon the sand of the sea, and saw a beast rise up out of the sea, having seven heads and ten horns, and upon his horns ten crowns, and upon his heads the name of blasphemy. And the beast which I saw was like unto a leopard, and his feet were as the feet of a bear, and his mouth as the mouth of a lion: and the dragon gave him his power, and his seat, and great authority. (Rev. 13:1,2)

The symbolic beasts mentioned in these verses encompass all the world empires of history and reveal the nature of the composite empire over which the beast or Antichrist will rule for three years. We have always taught that the Antichrist would come to power in the European area of the revived Roman Empire, according to Daniel chapters 2 and 7 and the thirteenth chapter of Revelation. Notice again what it says in the article quoted from *Europe Magazine*, "The sea has mapped out the way. Also, the Commission has chosen as its motto: "Making the SEA a success"

This is also the motto of the German presidency. The main goal is to create a free internal market in Europe by 1992 . . . It will improve the living conditions of people in Europe and consolidate the irreversible trend toward a European Union.

The European Parliament has been elected for the third time in 1989 from among the aggregate population of 320 million people. The European Monetary System (E.M.S.) is a priority project, and the European Currency Unit has worked very well as a stable currency and an alternative to the American dollar.

Already they are referring to the Common Market countries as the "Community" and in terms of its global responsibility. Also the Community wants to further develop its trilateral relations and trade agreements with Eastern European countries. Through the Council for Mutual Economic Assistance (COMECON) the E. C. is already associated with sixty-six African, Caribbean, and Pacific nations, an interesting figure in light of the thirteenth chapter of Revelation.

The eighth chapter of Daniel indicates that the Antichrist will come in with a global peace proposal but it does not produce any lasting peace, and the world will be plunged into a bloody war. I read with considerable interest what this illuminating article "Europe at the Crossroads" had to say about the European Community efforts to achieve global peace—page forty-six:

> The E.C.'s responsibility for peace is not confined to Europe. The Community will continue its stabilizing, peace-promoting efforts in the world's crisis-torn regions. This applies to the Gulf and to the Arab-Israeli conflicts, to Central America to South Africa and to Afghanistan. In the transition from bipolar to multipolar world, the dialogue with Japan and China is of eminent importance. The countries of the Middle East expect the E.C. to make constructive contributions. This includes efforts to bring about an international conference for which the Arab summit in Amman laid a significant basis.

The Eurotunnel linking the United Kingdom with the rest of Europe is scheduled for completion by 1993.

Quoting *Europe*, March 1988 page eighteen headlined "Eurotunnel Proceeds Despite Initial Capital Difficulties":

On February 5, British Prime Minister Margaret Thatcher did her bit for the Eurotunnel. At the controls of a $6.2 million boring machine, some 40 meters under the British Channel, Thatcher enthusiastically took the service tunnel of the 50 kilometer fixed link between England and France about one-half meter closer to the French tunnelers working on the other side. It is the final, personal identification of the Prime Minister with a project from which the government had initially remained at arm's length, refusing to inject government money or guarantees.

Inevitably, however, both the French and the British governments were involved. Thatcher's digging trip came just a year after the British and French jointly announced a scheme for "le plus gigantesque peace du monde." That was the way that Eurotunnel, the Anglo-French company, set up after due solemnities—a treaty signed in July 1987 by Thatcher and French president Francois Mitterrand endeavored to sell the [4.9-billion] project to the French public. To buy shares in the twin-bore rail tunnel to be built under the channel between southeast England and northwest France was, potential investors were told, to make a "rendezvous with history.

Although the Common Market is not yet all that its name implies, Jacques Delors, the president of the E. C. commission is working toward that goal by 1992, and believes that this project in common is altogether essential to world trade and competition with Japan and the United States.

Quoting *Europe*, March 1988, page sixteen:

Nineteen eighty-seven saw many changes in the U.S. export-controls field, and the groundwork was laid for what may be more in the months to come. While this opens many opportunities for the European Community, the E.C. also faces a number of challenges.

When the E.C. was formed, one of the basic ideas was to create one single market. However, despite the fact that many refer to the E.C. as the "Common Market," so far a really integrated market has not been achieved. The current E.C. Commission, and especially its president, Jacques Delors, decided that for Europe to meet the U.S. and Japanese challenge, a truly unified and integrated market had to be established soon. The completion of the internal market—in which the remaining barriers between the 12 member states are to be removed—is scheduled for the end of 1992."

Today in the European Community there are new maps of farming, forests, and a political map. An article (March 1988) on Nuclear Fusion Research in *Europe*, page twenty-six, aptly demonstrates that the European Community wants to be involved in all of the joint research and nuclear activities of the superpowers.

The article indicates to me that the European Economic Community aspires to become the world leader in research and development of nuclear power sources and the nuclear center of the nations. The Common Market countries are also striking new military postures as an article in *Europe* dated December 1987 demonstrates. The article is entitled "Europe Looks to Its Own Defense" and asserts that the

British military historian John Keegan, says that the past six months have shaken the Atlantic alliance more gravely than any other period in its 38-year existence.

There was a small tremor when former German Chancellor Helmut Schmidt suggested

that the Federal Republic of Germany effec-
tively put its troops in France's hands. In a
long letter to the West German weekly, DIE
/EIT, he argued: "Now is the time to replace
the 2O-year-old flexible response strategy
with a new approach-for example, by mass-
ing sufficient conventional forces through
the integration of German, French and
Benelux troops under a unified French command." Spelled out more simply, this comes
down to saying "let's see Europe shed its
nuclear dependency," and is a step toward
"Let's deal out the American hand at the
table." Today it is a European, not an
American, who is putting the crucial question most bluntly. Jean Pierre Bechter,
Secretary of the French Parliamentary
Committee on Defense, remarked lately, "Do
you think 320 million Europeans can continue forever to ask 240 million Americans
to defend us from 280 million Soviets?"

One of the most notable achievements of the Common
Market Entity is a more stable currency. We should all note
the success of the E.M.S. (European Monetary System) since
1979. Quoting *Europe*, December 1987, page twenty-two
"The European Monetary System—A Force for Stability
among Volatile Currency Markets":

Since the European Monetary System (EMS)
came into operation on March 13, 1979, the
countries of the European Community have
had to face a second oil price shock, a sus-
tained rise of the dollar and, since February
1985, a marked fall of the same currency.
Despite these unsettled international
conditions, the EMS has satisfactorily
answered its first purpose. This was to
establish close cooperation that would result
in a zone of monetary and price stability in
Europe.

However, even before 1979, we viewed the emergence of the "snake" as a kind of floating currency among the E. C. members. Continuing to quote:

> The first stage of this project began at the beginning of 1972. It consisted of restricting to approximately 2.25 percent the margin of fluctuation between European currencies. The currencies would remain linked to the dollar, with the similar margin. This system gave rise to the image of the "snake in the tunnel." A (EMCF) was set up, destined to be the embryo of a European central bank. To begin with, the EMCF had the task of managing the exchange mechanisms of the "snake" and its various credit arrangements.

The "Snake Currency" logically reminds us of the beast that comes up out of the sea (Rev 13:1, 2) and receives his power, his seat, and great authority from the dragon called that old serpent in the twelfth chapter of Revelation. The nature of the Antichrist economic system (see Rev 13:16,17) is similar to the European Currency Unit. A brief quotation from *Europe*, Dec 1987, page twenty-five, entitled "European Currency Unit Gains Favor" will demonstrate my point:

> The European Currency Unit (ECU), an exotic currency without coins or banknotes that some people think is a rare bird or a football star, is emerging in these days of shaky markets as a potential economic lifeline for Western Europe. With the dollar crumbling and faith in the U.S. economic leadership shaken by the Wall Street Crash, some bankers are pushing the ECU as the lynchpin of an integrated European economy. Visionaries who believe in a United States of Europe say the ECU, a national medium of financial transaction, should become the common currency in the European Community, a rival to the dollar

and a safeguard against today's volatile foreign exchange movements.

With the E. C. U. doing so well among the community of twelve, the falling dollar will probably never again be the currency standard for the Common Market.

You can readily see how the European Community, having come of age in 1987, is now flaunting its composite muscles politically, militarily, and economically. Europe has also joined the space race and now strives to be number one. Europe's space officials have spent more than two years working out detailed plans for providing Europe with a space program that would give it independence from the United States. In fact, an article in *Europe* Magazine December 1987 is headlined "Europe Moves Toward Full Autonomy in Space."

It is evident that God has finally permitted the Roman Empire to be revived in our generation. The thrilling fact that causes Christians to rejoice is the scheduled event that must take place when the Revived Roman Empire is in full view. "And in the days of these kings shall the God of Heaven set up a kingdom, which shall never be destroyed: and the kingdom shall not be left to other people, but it shall break in pieces and consume all these kingdoms, and it shall stand for ever" (Dan. 2:44).

According to the common market nations, and their own official pronouncements in their monthly magazine, *Europe*, 1992 is their target date to have complete unity in every area of the confederacy of the United States of Europe. By this established date, the image should be intact.

Eleven

THE IMAGE OF JEALOUSY

The title for this chapter comes from one of Ezekiel's visions which God gave him concerning apostasy and idolatry among the religious leaders of Judah. Ezekiel chapter 8 is a very revealing indictment against the ecclesiastical hierarchy of Ezekiel's time, and a prophetic picture of the religious system for the last days:

> And it came to pass in the sixth year, in the sixth month, in the fifth day of the month, as I sat in mine house, and the elders of Judah sat before me, that the hand of the Lord God fell there upon me. Then I beheld, and lo a likeness as the appearance of fire: from the appearance of his loins even downward, fire; and from his loins even up-ward, as the appearance of brightness, as the colour of amber. And he put forth the form of an hand, and took me by a lock of mine head; and the spirit lifted me up between the earth and the heaven, and brought me in the visions of God to Jerusalem, to the door of the inner gate that looketh toward the north; where was the seat of the image of jealousy, which provoketh to jealousy. (Ezek. 8:1-3)

Now why does God call this seat or altar an "image of Jealousy"? Because God will not share His glory with another god, "Worship God," "Him only shalt thou serve."

The children of Israel knew all about this, since the time of the Law, it has been revealed. "Thou shalt have no other gods before me. Thou shalt not make unto thee any graven image, or any likeness of anything that is in heaven above, or that is in the earth beneath, or that is in the water under the earth" (Exod. 20:3-4).

As we study certain passages in Ezekiel chapter 8, we can determine that the image of jealousy was some kind of abominable idol before which the elders of Judah bowed down. We also discover that these religious leaders were involved in occult practices, astrology, and witchcraft.

It is apparent that the ancients of Judah were worshipping the false gods of the Canaanites; the sun, moon, and stars (as in the horoscope), abominable beasts of mythology, and all kinds of witchcraft.

In the book of Ezekiel we read:

> Then said he unto me, Son of man, lift up thine eyes now the way toward the north. So I lifted up mine eyes the way toward the north, and behold northward at the gate of the altar this image of jealousy in the entry. He said furthermore unto me, Son of man, seest thou what they do? Even the great abominations that the house of Israel committeth here, that I should go far off from my sanctuary? But turn thee yet again, and thou shalt see greater abominations. And he brought me to the door of the court; and when I looked, behold a hole in the wall. Then he said unto me, Son of man dig now in the wall; and when I had digged in the wall, behold a door. And he said unto me, Go in, and behold the wicked abominations that they do here. So I went in and saw; and behold every form of creeping things, and abominable beasts, and all the idols of the house of Israel, portrayed upon the wall round about. And there stood before them

seventy men of the ancients of the house of Israel, and In the midst of them stood Jazaniah the son of Shaphan, with every man his censer in his hand; and a thick cloud of incense went up.

This image of jealousy was set up at the northern gate—probably the Damascus gate. This part of old Jerusalem is honeycombed with caves and tunnels.

To impress upon you how Satan is reviving these images and symbols, I refer to Tex Marr's best-selling book, *Mystery Mark of the New Age*, chapter 5 "The Unholy Worship of the Symbols of Oppression":

> A flood of new and strange, yet ancient and archaic, symbols is overflowing America and the world. Watch the ads on television for just one night, especially on the rock music channel, or kids' Saturday cartoon shows, or read three or four popular magazines and look for the symbols. You'll be amazed. We are literally deluged with satanic symbols—with pentagrams, triangles, rainbows, perverted crosses, pyramids, and more.
>
> The Images are usually presented to us either in a subtle, indirect way or up front in a positive manner. Rarely are we given the impression that there is anything wrong with these images. "*THE HIDDEN DANGER OF SYMBOL THERAPY*"—"Modern psychiatry actually fosters and supports the New Age in its insidious campaign to spread far and wide the dangerously malignant symbols of Satan. Dick Sutphen, a hypnotist whose human potential seminars have probably been attended by tens of thousands, has even been successful in promoting what the New Age calls "Symbol Therapy."

Sutphen's tape company, Valley of the Sun, has produced a series of six videotapes which bombard the viewer's mind with what is termed "Therapeutic symbols." Sutphen says that Symbol Therapy will change your life, and he writes: "Symbol Therapy uses powerful and effective superconscious visualizations, which can have positive, rejuvenative mental and physical effects. Symbol Therapy works by restructuring and redirecting certain unconscious energies ... [Symbol Therapy] relaxes your body, then directs you through the beautiful visualizations ..."

I believe that Sutphen, being a professional hypnotist, knows full well that the combination of intense visual imagery—"Symbol Therapy"—and the mesmerizing nature of New Age mood music will charm like a snake. It will turn the New Age victim into a pliant and submissive zombie whose mind is totally under bondage to Satan.

Of course, this is just what Sutphen desires. It should be noted that he and his wife Tara (the same name as one of the Greek Mother Goddesses!) head a group called Reincarnationist, Inc. This group is dedicated to combatting Christian fundamentalists.

Unfortunately, many of these occult practices like journaling (spirit writing) and visualization or imaging, are coming right into our mainline denominational churches. For example: quoting John Bareia's excellent book, *Antichrist Associates*, chapter 9, "Mysticism within Christian Organizations," page 136:

Occult classes taught in churches—Mainline Protestant churches—are also taking part in allowing occult practices to come into their sanctuaries, seminars and Sunday

Schools. We found that many so-called Christian churches were willing to open their doors to certain classes which are clearly of the occult. For instance, one Methodist Church in Tulsa recently offered a "Meditation and Journaling" workshop. According to their brochure, "Participants will use Scripture, meditation, guided imagery and writing to take themselves on a journey through seven dimensions of the spirit life."

A class schedule from the Tulsa Learning Community shows several other churches in the city were willing to open their doors to esoteric classes as well. One class on yoga meditation was being held at a Presbyterian church. Another class, on handwriting analysis, is being held at a Christian church.

How can this be? II Corinthians 11:3-4 clearly says, "But I fear, lest by any means, as the serpent beguiled Eve through his subtlety, so your minds should be corrupted from the simplicity that is in Christ. For if he that comes preaches another Jesus, whom we have not preached, or if you receive another spirit, which you have not received, or another gospel which you have not accepted, you might well bear with them"

In his book entitled, *The Potential Principle*, Edwin Louis Cole writes: "One of the most important things you can do in life is create an image. Now according to the Bible, the second commandment is, Thou shalt not make unto yourselves any graven Images. Yet here is this man who states that one of the most important things you can do is create an image.

But, even worse, this author cites Psalms

115:4-8 to back up his beliefs: "Their idols (or images) are silver and gold, the work of men's hands. They have mouths, but they speak not; eyes have they, but they see not; They have ears, but they hear not; noses have they, but they smell not; They have hands, but they handle not; feet have they, but they walk not; neither speak they through their throat. They that make them are like unto them. So is everyone that trusteth In them."

Once again, I would like to emphasize the fact that today, the image is the thing. In business, politics, religion, or whatever it might be, the image is the all important thing. Everything revolves around your public or corporate image. This also holds true in the rapidly expanding world of electronics. In the burgeoning world of computer networking, Imaging is the most innovative area of this twentieth century science.

Imaging is also a new age distinctive and is essential to meditating and channeling. Man's image is also the central thrust of secular Humanism, promoting man's sinful image rather than God's holy image. You could even call it the battle of the images. And this battle will be decisively ended when Jesus Christ ("the express image of God" Hebrews 1:3) returns to this planet to smash the image of the beast or Antichrist at Armageddon.

There has been a great unprecedented revival in the daily horoscope and the signs of the Zodiac. Today the daily horoscope is carried in more than two thousand daily newspapers and reflects the interest of modern man in directing his own destiny by the stars. It also demonstrates how modern man is once again worshipping the sun, the moon, and the stars. This was the final abomination and accusation that God brings against the elders of Judah in Ezekiel:

Then said he unto me, Son of Man, hast thou seen what the ancients of the house of Israel do in the dark, every man in the chambers of

his imagery? For they say, The Lord seeth us
not; the Lord hath forsaken the earth. He said
also unto me, Turn thee yet again, and thou
shalt see greater abominations that they do.

Then he brought me to the door of the gate
of the Lord's house which was toward the
north; and, behold, there sat women
weeping for Tammuz.

Then said he unto me, Hast thou seen this, 0
son of Man? Turn thee yet again, and thou
shalt see greater abominations than these.
And he brought me into the inner court of
the Lord's house, and, behold, at the door of
the temple of the Lord, between the porch
and the altar, were about five and twenty
men, with their backs toward the temple of
the Lord, and their faces toward the east; and
they worshiped the sun toward the east.
(Ezek. 8:12-16)

The chambers of imagery are much in use today as
individuals and entire families spend hour upon hour
viewing images upon the television screen, or watching
video-tapes and pornographic movies. God's judgment will
surely fall upon those who prefer the devil's message above
the living and abiding word of God.

The women weeping for Tammuz (verse 14) were the
followers of the Queen of heaven, Semiramis (Tammuz's
mother), the wife of Nimrod, the post-flood rebel and
mighty hunter of the souls of men. Nimrod was evidently
the originator of astrology, the corruption of God's Bible in
the Heavens. Evidence of these manmade images abound
in the ruins of the ancient Tower of Babel.

Notice in verses fifteen and sixteen the priests had
turned their backs upon God's house, the Temple, and were
worshipping the sun, like the pagan people of that land. In
many places, God says that He will judge such abominations as worshipping the "stars, the sun and the moon," and

looking to these heavenly lights for blessing and prosperity rather than to God.

> I will also stretch out mine hand upon Judah, and upon all the inhabitants of Jerusalem; and I will cut off the remnant of Baal from this place, and the name of the Chemarim with the priests; And them that worship the host of heaven upon the housetops; and them that worship and that swear by the Lord, and that swear by Malcham. (Zech. 1:4-5)

Witchcraft is continually and categorically condemned in the Bible.

> And when they shall say unto you, Seek unto them that have familiar spirits, and unto wizards that peep, and that mutter: should not a people seek unto their God or the living to the dead? To the law and to the testimony; if they speak not according to this word, it is because there is no light in them. And they shall look unto the earth; and behold trouble and darkness, dimness of anguish; and they shall be driven to darkness. (Isa. 8:19-20,22)

In the 1960s promiscuity brought herpes as a judgment of God upon that rebellious generation. In the 1980s, homosexuals came out of the closet and God sent a more fearful judgment upon our nation, the fatal disease of AIDS. As we begin the unknown decade of the 1990s, all apocalyptic signs indicate that the fearful events predicted in God's holy word are converging upon the world scene; and God's timetable may well run its course in the final decade of this century.

As witches and sorcery come out of the closet, more fearful judgments will fall upon this world of increasing darkness. To demonstrate how fast these prophecies are paralleling today's world, I will quote *Prophecy in the News*, November 1988, a revealing article by J.R. Church, "Witches and Pagans in Le Army:"

In a recent issue of a military newspaper called *Army Times*, we came across an article by Grant Willis. Mr. Willis has interviewed members of the military who practice witchcraft and paganism. They tell him that they are tired of living in secrecy. They want to emerge into society and gain the respect that they think they deserve.

Signs of their new assertiveness appeared (last fall) in Europe, when some witches and pagans formed a network called the Far-wander Military Pagan Fellowship. Air Force Staff Sergeant Lorie A. Johnson said she placed an announcement in *European Stars And Stripes* to recruit fellow members.

"The goal is to let military pagans know they're not alone," Johnson said, and "to show the military that we're not just a bunch of scattered weirdos."

As Mr. Willis talked with his pagan inter-viewees, they informed him that they are simply people who believe in more than one god. Some call themselves "Wiccans." [The word "witch" by the way, comes from this term.] They further told him that theirs is a tribal form of worship based on magic, her-bology, healing and the worship of the "Mother Goddess," and her consort the "Horned God." This information, he dis-covered, is also printed in the 1978 Army Chaplain's Handbook.

Pagans, he was told, are quick to point out that they do not worship the devil, which they believe to be only a Judeo-Christian concept. Air Force Technical Sergeant Rik Johnson told Willis that he became a witch some sixteen years ago. John told him that Wiccan ceremonies take place by candlelight because electricity blunts psychic energies. A ritual blunt knife, called an "atheme," is pointed during some ceremonies. It focuses the energies, he said, "like a psychic laser."

At the climax of an emotional ceremony, which includes meditation, dancing and speaking in tongues, energy is supposedly directed for a specific purpose. Some covens reportedly hold their ceremonies in the nude and engage in sexual orgies. Willis noted that several pagans told him that they reject Christian concepts of "sin" and enjoy their religion's emphasis on guilt-free celebration of natural urges.

And so it goes, as we lurch toward the glorious "New Age." Even our military has been invaded by the pagan practice of sorcery and goddess worship. Once again, we see all too clearly that there is no institution in our society that is immune to the encroachment of Satanic power.

The image of jealousy will again be set up in Jerusalem; only this time, it will be the real thing. In chapter 8 of *Mystery Mark of the New Age*, Texe Marrs talks about "The Image That Lives and Speaks!" and the master image. His description of the coming image of the beast closely parallels our interpretation. Under the heading "Bible Prophecy and the Image", page 137 he relates:

Bible prophecy tells us that the Image of the Beast will actually live and speak. It is possible today, through laser holography technology, to create an image of light that can move and speak as if alive. Indeed, this has been demonstrated. I have written about this amazing new high-tech development previously, and I have written several books on robots. With advanced computer brains and artificial intelligence software, a robot can "come alive"; it can walk, talk, see, hear, even smell!

It is conceivable that the Image of the Beast could be a laser holographic image or perhaps a robot that New Age priests and ministers someday will set up in churches and temples throughout the world. All would be forced to worship this image, since it would represent the Beast himself.

The image of jealousy or the image of the Beast will again be set up at Jerusalem and as this sinister computerized image is promoted worldwide by means of fiber optics, satellites and cable, the counterfeit Christ will endeavor to subdue all the world under his feet, and impose his distinctive mark upon every living soul. May God speak to many hearts to flee to the rock of ages, the Lord Jesus Christ, for salvation and cleansing from sin in order that they may escape God's fearful wrath and judgment that will surely be poured out upon this "Image of Jealousy" and all who bow down before it.

Twelve

THE IMAGE OF JUDGMENT

"**S**o He made man in the image of God; in the image of God made He them." Yet man, throughout the ages, has set about to make a GOD in the image of MAN. From the image in Daniel until this very day, man expends vast amounts of time, energy, money and talent in the search to make something in his own image that he can worship. And as each one is made, man has bowed before the latest "image" as though it were God.

Statues of men, photographs, television, robots—all are images of man. As the centuries have passed, man has worshipped and followed heroes—often they have been military leaders but sometimes they are political, artistic, philosophical, ideological or other kinds of leaders. Pictures that came out of China during the leadership of Mao Tse Tung showed his picture on billboards, banners, books, and everywhere the citizens of that country looked.

But, in spite of all the differences in these "images of man," there is one great similarity. They all come to the same end as represented by the image in Daniel. We read in the book of Daniel:

> Thou sawest till that a stone was cut out
> without hands, which smote the image upon
> his feet that were of iron and clay, and break
> them to pieces. Then was the iron, the clay,
> the brass, the silver, and the gold broken to

> pieces together, and became like the chaff of
> the summer threshing floors; and the wind
> carried them away, that no place was found
> for them; and the stone that smote the image
> became a great mountain, and filled the
> whole earth. (Dan. 2:34-35)

The "stone cut out without hands" is the eternal Rock of Ages. From the time that Moses struck the rock in the wilderness and water gushed forth to satisfy the thirst of the children of Israel, until Jesus reminded the chief priests and elders that "the stone which the builders rejected has become the chief cornerstone," Jesus has been the Rock. And it's true in Daniel. The rock that smites the iron and clay feet of the image and breaks them to pieces is none other than God, Himself, judging the nations. "Of the Rock that begat thee thou art unmindful and hast forgotten God that formed thee" (Deut. 32:18).

I stand in amazement as I read that Lucifer, Son of the Morning, said, "I will be like the Most High." But mankind has been saying the same thing through the annals of time; indeed, man has usually gone further and said, "I will *be* the Most High" and then erected his own image to worship—"unmindful of the God that formed" him.

Do I hear an argument that the public doesn't actually "worship" these images? Do young people "worship" rock stars? Most churches would be shaken to their foundation if the people of God worshipped God with the same fervor that the youth of the world scream, wave and gyrate to identify with their "heroes"! Their clothes must be just as the singers' clothes! No matter how strange or unacceptable to those close to them, their hair must be combed (or not combed) just as their heroes. Isn't this worship? Of course it is.

The average adult doesn't fall into this trap, however. But, what about the hours and hours spent in front of the television set whether or not there is anything of interest or of value being shown? What is the first thing you do when you arrive home from work? Do you turn on the lights first or the television set? What do you see there? Images! Oh yes, you *need* to know what's going on in the world.

But do the expert anchormen *really* tell you? Or do they set themselves up as some kind of expert whether or not their opinion is backed up by any kind of expertise. Are these "experts" chosen on the basis of their wisdom and insight? Or are they there because they project the "right" image to the television camera? Much of what we think and believe is what we hear and see on TV. It would be far better to get our point of view from God's Word!

God's Word says:

> And the times of this ignorance God winked at; but now commandeth all men everywhere to repent; Because he hath appointed a day, in the which he will judge the world in righteousness by that man whom he hath ordained: whereof he hath given assurance unto all men, in that he hath raised him from the dead. (Acts 17:30-31)

God is holy and perfectly righteous. He must send judgment on sin or He would not be God. God will judge the nations just as the stone broke the feet of the image in Daniel. Did you notice? When the image fell, it was broken into such fine dust that the wind carried away the metals which had formed the image. Even a small nugget of gold is not blown away by the wind—but the iron, silver, brass and gold of the statue are ground into dust so fine that the wind blows them away! This demonstrates to us the extent of God's judgment on sin. Those whom God judges cannot even be found; He grinds them into dust so fine that the wind carries them away and "no place is found for them." Consider the judgment of God!

Historically, Babylon was judged by the Medes and the Persians and yet, in recent years, we have again seen Babylon and Persia with the contemporary names of Iraq and Iran, fighting yet another costly war where children and young men are sacrificed on the altar of political expediency. We hear with interest, the reports that Babylon is being rebuilt to grandeur as it was in the days of Nebuchadnezzar. Recently, Babylon held an international music festival to show the world that Babylon is alive and well.

But in describing the last days, the book of Revelation tells us:

> And after these things I saw another angel come down from heaven, having great power; and the earth was lightened with his glory. And he cried mightily with a strong voice, saying, Babylon the great is fallen, is fallen, and is become the habitation of devils, and the hold of every foul spirit, and a cage of every unclean and hateful bird. For all nations have drunk of the wine of the wrath of her fornication and the kings of the earth have committed fornication with her, and the merchants of the earth are waxed rich through the abundance of her delicacies. And I heard another voice from heaven, saying, Come out of her, my people, that ye receive not of her plagues. For her sins have reached unto heaven, and God hath remembered her iniquities. (Rev. 18:1-5)

This passage presents a picture in which Babylon, where the occult was born and grew into prominence, will again be the location from where occult activity will concentrate and emanate. But, in the last days, Babylon and the occult will be decisively and finally judged. In her book, *The Prophets Identify the USA and Foretell Her Destiny*, author Della Sue Collins says on page twenty-two:

> Almost hidden, but revealed by the Spirit of God, is an application in Isaiah 13 to the end time Babylon. Immediately after describing the restoration of Israel and the coming of the Messiah, followed by singing praises to God in chapters 11 and 12, Babylon was conquered by the Medes and Persians, but the land of ancient Babylon, which is present

day Iraq, is located on the Euphrates River and is still inhabited. Ancient Babylon was not totally destroyed by the Medes and Persians. In fact, remember that, after the Medo-Persian empire was established, upon conquering Babylon in 538 B.C., Daniel was made an official under Darius who ruled over the Babylonian realm of the Medo-Persian Empire. To this day, the area where early Babylon was located is, in fact, still inhabited.

But what does Isaiah 13 say? "And Babylon, the glory of kingdoms, the beauty of the Chaldees' excellency, shall be as when God overthrew Sodom and Gomorrah. It shall never be inhabited, neither shall the Arabian pitch tent there . . . But wild beasts of the desert shall lie there . . . And the wild beasts of the islands shall cry in their desolate houses . . . and her time is near to come, and her days shall not be prolonged." The Babylon pictured here had her roots from the Chaldeans who founded the occult practice of paganism and luciferian worship; but this Babylon is the end time Babylon with its headquarters located at the same place where the last one world system is centered.

To help better understand the destruction herein described of this Babylon, the glory of the kingdoms or the most powerful of all world kingdoms, we must look at how Sodom and Gomorrah were destroyed. In Deuteronomy 29:33, "And that the whole land thereof is brimstone and salt, and burning, and that it is not sown, nor beareth, nor any grass groweth therein, like the overthrew of Sodom and Gomorrah, which the Lord overthrew in his anger, and in his wrath." This end time Babylon will be completely destroyed by burning.

Why were Sodom and Gomorrah destroyed? They were destroyed because of the wickedness of the people. Immorality was the code by which they lived. Remember first comes idolatry, the worship of false gods; then comes immorality; and finally comes perversion such as homosexuality, incest, and child molestation. Sodom and Gomorrah were filled with homosexuality and to this day, the word sodomy still gives reference to this depravity of man at his lowest level.

And so, Isaiah identifies that end time Babylon with the occult practices of Chaldea who was also the originator of the sexagesimal numerical system and deleted the 0; the system is based on the number six. Six is the number of man. Man was created on the sixth day. Satan's number is 666. In the Holy Bible, six is the number of imperfection, with seven the number of completion or perfection. Therefore, we know that this end time Babylon will be destroyed by burning as the Hebrew prophets have all predicted.

When this Babylon is destroyed, it will have surpassed the decadence of Sodom and Gomorrah. End time Babylon will be a nation where homosexuality is both prevalent and approved by its population. It will be a nation wherein the Chaldean numerical system will have a revived state with a base of six and a constant use of the number 666, Satan's number.

Notice the apocalyptic judgments in Isaiah chapter 13 and the link to the end-time Babylon:

> Behold the day of the Lord cometh, cruel
> both with wrath and fierce anger, to lay the
> land desolate: and he shall destroy the sin-
> ners thereof out of it. For the stars of heaven
> and the constellations thereof shall not give
> their light; the sun shall be darkened in his
> going forth, and the moon shall not cause her
> light to shine. And I will punish the world
> for their evil and the wicked for their iniq-
> uity; and I will cause the arrogancy of the
> proud to cease, and will lay low the haughti-
> ness of the terrible. I will make a man more
> precious than fine gold; even a man than the
> golden wedge of Ophir. Therefore I will
> shake the heavens, and the earth shall
> remove out of her place, in the wrath of the
> Lord of hosts, and in the day of his fierce
> anger. And Babylon, the glory of kingdoms,
> the beauty of the Chaldees' excellency, shall
> be as when God overthrew Sodom and
> Gomorrah. It shall never be inhabited,
> neither shall it be dwelt in from generation
> to generation; neither shall the Arabian pitch
> tent there; neither shall the shepherds make
> their fold there. But wild beasts of the desert
> shall lie there; and their houses shall be full
> of doleful creatures; and owls shall dwell
> there, and Satyrs shall dance there. And the
> wild beasts of the islands shall cry in their
> desolate houses, and dragons in their
> pleasant palaces; and her time is near to
> come, and her days shall not be prolonged.
> (Isa. 13:9-13, 19-22)

To determine how God destroyed Sodom and Gomor-
rah and the cities of the plains, we go to the book of Genesis.
We discover that God destroyed Sodom and Gomorrah in
one day by a fiery judgment from heaven:

> The sun was risen upon the earth when Lot
> entered into Zoar. Then the Lord rained

> upon Sodom and upon Gomorrah
> brimstone and fire from the Lord out of
> heaven; and he overthrew those cities and all
> the plain, and all the inhabitants of the cities,
> and that which grew upon the ground. But
> his wife looked back from behind him, and
> she became a pillar of salt. And Abraham gat
> up early in the morning to the place where
> he stood before the Lord: And he looked
> toward Sodom and Gomorrah, and toward
> all the land of the plain, and beheld, and, lo,
> the smoke of the country went up as the
> smoke of a furnace. (Gen. 19:23-28)

In like manner will God destroy the end-time Babylon by fire and brimstone out of heaven. But there is another end-time power to be considered in the alignment of nations for the last days, in light of God's prophetic timetable. This is the mystery woman of Revelation chapter 17 described as Mystery Babylon. Clarence Larkin, who studies prophecy and wrote a tremendous book, *Dispensational Truth* held to the position of *Two Babylons*. Quoting Dispensational Truth, page 140,

> That the ancient city of Babylon restored is
> to play an important part in the startling
> events of the last days of this Dispensation,
> is very clear. This is seen from what is said
> of it in the seventeenth and eighteenth chap-
> ters of the book of Revelation. At first sight
> the two chapters, which contain some things
> in common, are difficult to reconcile, but
> when we get the "key" the reconciliation is
> easy.

> The 17th chapter speaks of a "woman" and
> this "woman" is called MYSTERY
> BABYLON THE GREAT, THE MOTHER OF
> HARLOTS AND ABOMINATIONS OF
> THE EARTH. The 18th chapter speaks of a
> "City," a literal city, called "Babylon the

Great" that the "woman" and the "City" do
not symbolize the same thing is clear, for
what is said of the "woman" does not apply
to a city, and what is said of the "City" does
not   apply to a woman. The "woman" is
destroyed by the "Ten   Kings" while the
"kings of the earth" in the next chapter, "Be-
wail and lament" a mighty earthquake and
fire. Again the "Woman" is destroyed three
and a half years before the city; and the fact
that the first verse of chapter 18 says, "After
these things" that is after the destruction of
the "woman" That the woman and the "city"
are not one and the same.

Chapter 17 of the Revelation presents to us the picture
of a brazen and gaudy harlot. She is designated "Mystery
Babylon the Great, the Mother of harlots and abominations
of the earth." With such a title, Mystery Babylon must have
had a long and notorious history. For to be the "mother" of
abominations and harlots argues conclusively that she was
before, and gave birth to, that which answers to abominations and harlotries.

Edward Tracy in his excellent book, *The United States in
Prophecy*, discusses the background and characteristic of
this mystery woman of Revelation 17:

Those who have even a little acquaintance
with the Old   Testament will at once
recognize these figures of speech as being
used by the God of Israel to describe that
nation when it gave itself over to heathen
forms of worship. Israel was said to have
"played the harlot with many lovers." That
is, she had embraced the many pagan gods
of the nations round about her (Jeremiah
3:1). In the first verse of chapter 4 of
Jeremiah, the idols and idolatrous practices
of Israel are called abominations.

It has come to be common knowledge that all forms of

paganism can be traced to the same foul source. In his book, *The Two Babylons*, Alexander Hislop has painstakingly traced the source of all heathen forms of worship to ancient Babel. There is no hint of idolatry in the Bible records before the flood. So-called civilization had its birthplace in ancient Babel under the leadership of Nimrod and his dissolute wife, Semiramis. You will recall that it was at Babel that God confused the tongues of the inhabitants and formed the nations.

America is a great nation, just over two hundred years old. In spite of our tremendous heritage, we have manifested Babel-like characteristics from the very beginning, as a melting pot of nationalities and an open door policy for immigration. English, our official language has virtually become the universal tongue.

To demonstrate how far removed our beloved nation, America, is from its glorious heritage and spectacular conception, consider one of the New Age trends at the Pentagon. "President Reagan's Strategic Defense Initiative isn't the only SDI program afoot in the corridors of power," according to *The Washington Post*, March 23, 1988, which ran an article entitled, "A New Aura Begins at Pentagon."

> Members of the Pentagon Meditation Club hope to deploy a spiritual "peace shield" around the planet through what they call their "Spiritual Defense Initiative."
>
> The club, a private association of fifteen Department of Defense employees from civilian technicians to military officers, gathers every Friday at its "spiritual command post" inside the Pentagon to project mental messages of peace and love.
>
> "Years ago, I always thought, Well, the military is nothing but war," said Clarence Wright, 42, a club member who works at the Pentagon as a copier technician. "But I began to realize there's a lot more than that going on at the Pentagon."

"It may be the secret weapon that we will need in order to replace the nuclear threat," said Ed Winchester, president of the club, which has been active in various forms since 1976. Winchester, said an individual's shield can be measured by a hand-held device called a "peace shield gauge" that resembles a water dowser. The club sells them for $65 apiece.

The night that President Reagan ordered a doubling of US troop strength in Honduras, Winchester used his gauge to determine whether any peaceful vibrations were radiating from the Pentagon, he said. "The first reading taken near the Pentagon flag-pole, was surprisingly strong—a clear indication," Winchester said, "that peace shield meditation was at work inside."

He got another solid reading on the Pentagon from the north parking lot. "I thought, well, it is conceivable that the amount of spiritual energy radiating from this source could go over the entire city."

"The energy is bubbling up," said Winchester. "It's happening. More than 200 Pentagon employees have been trained in peace shield meditation."

"See it radiating out into the hallways of the Pentagon, throughout the building, expanding to include the entire city and the nation, and reaching to every military installation, military personnel around the world—particularly to the Palmerola Air Force Base in Honduras."

When he is meditating, Walter Benesch, a 39-year-old civilian management analyst in the office of the Secretary of Defense, trains the psychic energy within his body on a mental image of the Earth spinning on its axis. For an added "power boost," Benesch envisions the Earth surrounded by symbols that are significant to him—the compass and square of the international Freemasons society. For high-ranking military officers too embarrassed to attend Pentagon Meditation Club meetings, the club sells $70 home meditation kits that include a 90-page manual and three 1-hour cassettes that instruct the listener in the fine points of meditation.

God will judge the United States for worshipping the occult in place of worshipping God. The initial blessings enjoyed in this country because of the faith of our forefathers will not protect us from the judgement of God on our sin today.

But I would be remiss if I did not mention one last and most important point to be drawn from Daniel's image (and all the other images of man) and God's judgment upon it.

The Bible, as well as historical and archeological evidence, shows that Daniel survived the invasion of the Medes and the Persians and was placed in positions of honor for many years after that time. Not everyone is destroyed by the judgments of God—for some there is salvation, escape from destruction and blessing bestowed AFTER God judges sin. How can that happen? Does God miss some that deserve judgment? Is sin "excused" in some while it is judged in everyone else?

In every warning of judgment God gives, He also offers safety and protection for those who will come to Him and obey Him—those who will love His Word and live by His truth. These blessings are not based on the "image of man"— it doesn't matter what you look like. God's blessings are offered solely on the attitude of your heart.

Daniel survived and was catapulted to power after the destruction of the image because his heart was right before God. He believed what God had said no matter what the astrologers and soothsayers were teaching. When the flood was to come, God warned Noah and told him to build an ark. Noah, in spite of how it looked to his neighbors, built a boat many miles from water even though it had never before rained on the earth. Noah's belief in what God said was what saved him and his family.

Even compromising Lot was warned to get out of Sodom before God's judgment fell. He wasn't an exemplary believer, but he was a righteous man and God remembered to warn him, too. He left the city and was saved from God's judgment.

As we consider our world today and the truth of God's Word, the prophecies of the end times and the wickedness we can see all around us, we too must know that God's judgment cannot be far away. Television, robots in human form, computers with artificial intelligence—all of these are the epitome of "the image of man" and the world has fallen at their feet to worship them as the "wave of the future."

But God says that the future only holds judgment for man. Yet, as always, He offers salvation to those who will believe His Word and follow Him. Jesus is not only a "stone of stumbling and a rock of offense," He is also the Rock of Ages and the Chief Cornerstone!

> Oh safe to the Rock that is higher than I
> My soul in its conflict and sorrow would fly.
> So sinful, so weary, Thine, Thine would I be.
> Oh, blest Rock of Ages, I'm hiding in Thee.
> How oft' in the conflict when pressed by the foe
> I have fled to my Refuge and breathed out my woe!
> How often when sorrows like sea billows roll
> Have I hidden in Thee, oh Thou Rock of my soul.
> Hiding in Thee, Hiding in Thee,
> Thou blest Rock of Ages, I'm hiding in Thee.

MORE GOOD BOOKS FROM HUNTINGTON HOUSE PUBLISHERS

Kinsey, Sex and Fraud: The Indoctrination of a People
by Dr. Judith A. Reisman and Edward Eichel

Kinsey, Sex and Fraud describes the research of Alfred Kinsey which shaped Western society's beliefs and understanding of the nature of human sexuality. His unchallenged conclusions are taught at every level of education—elementary, highschool and college—and quoted in textbooks as undisputed truth.

The authors clearly demonstrate that Kinsey's research involved illegal experimentations on several hundred children. The survey was carried out on a non-representative group of Americans, including disproportionately large numbers of sex offenders, prostitutes, prison inmates and exhibitionists.

ISBN 0-910311-20-X $19.95 Hard cover

Seduction of the Innocent Revisited by John Fulce

You honestly can't judge a book by its cover—especially a comic book! Comic books of yesteryear bring to mind cute cartoon characters, super-heroes battling the forces of evil or a sleuth tracking down the bad guy clue-by-clue. But that was a long, long time ago.

Today's comic books aren't innocent at all! Author John Fulce asserts that "super-heroes" are constantly found in the nude engaging in promiscuity, and satanic symbols are abundant throughout the pages. Fulce says most parents aren't aware of the contents of today's comic books—of what their children are absorbing from these seemingly innocent forms of entertainment. As a comic book collector for many years, Fulce opened his own comic book store in 1980, only to sell the business a few short years later due to the steady influx of morally unacceptable material. What's happening in the comic book industry? Fulce outlines the moral, biblical, and legal aspects and proves his assertions with page after page of illustrations. We need to pay attention to what our children are reading, Fulce claims. Comic books are not as innocent as they used to be.

ISBN 0-910311-66-8 $8.95

Dinosaurs and the Bible by David W. Unfred

Every reader, young and old, will be fascinated by this ever-mysterious topic—exactly what happened to the dinosaurs? Author David Unfred draws a very descriptive picture of the history and fate of the dinosaurs, using the Bible as a reference guide.

In this educational and informative book, Unfred answers such questions as: Did dinosaurs really exist? Does the Bible mention dinosaurs? What happened to dinosaurs, or are there some still living awaiting discovery? Unfred uses the Bible to help unlock the ancient mysteries of the lumbering creatures, and teaches how those mysteries can educate us about God the Creator and our God of Love.

ISBN 0-910311-70-6 $12.95 Hard cover

ORDER THESE BOOKS FROM HUNTINGTON HOUSE PUBLISHERS!

_____ America Betrayed—Marlin Maddoux __ __ __ __ __	$6.95	_____
_____ Backward Masking Unmasked—Jacob Aranza __ __ __	6.95	_____
_____ Deadly Deception: Freemasonry—Tom McKenney _____	7.95	_____
_____ Delicate Balance—John Zajac __ __ __ __ __ __ __	8.95	_____
_____ Devil Take The Youngest—Winkie Pratney __ __ __ __	8.95	_____
The Devil's Web—Pat Pulling with Kathy Cawthon		
_____	Trade paper _____	8.95	_____
_____	Hard cover _____	16.95	_____
_____ •Dinosaurs and the Bible—Dave Unfred __ __ __ __ __	12.95	_____
_____ Exposing the AIDS Scandal—Dr. Paul Cameron __ __	7.95	_____
_____ From Rock to Rock—Eric Barger __ __ __ __ __ __	8.95	_____
•God's Rebels—Henry Lee Curry III, Ph.D.		
_____	Trade paper _____	12.95	_____
_____	Hard cover_____	21.95	_____
The Hidden Dangers of the Rainbow—		
	Constance Cumbey__ __	8.95	_____
_____ Inside the New Age Nightmare—Randall Baer__ __ __	8.95	_____
_____ Jubilee on Wall Street—David Knox Barker__ __ __	7.95	_____
•Kinsey, Sex and Fraud—Dr. Judith A. Reisman &		
_____	Edward Eichel __ __ __ __ __	19.95	_____
_____ Last Days Collection—Last Days Ministries __ __ __	8.95	_____
_____•Lord! Why Is My Child A Rebel?—Jacob Aranza __ __	6.95	_____
_____ Lucifer Connection—Joseph Carr__ __ __ __ __ __	7.95	_____
•New World Order: The Ancient Plan of Secret Societies—		
_____	William T. Still __ __ __	8.95	_____
_____ Personalities in Power—Florence Littauer __ __ __ __	8.95	_____
_____ A Reasonable Reason To Wait—Jacob Aranza __ __ __	5.95	_____
_____•Seduction of the Innocent Revisited—John Fulce _____	8.95	_____
•Soft Porn Plays Hardball—Dr. Judith A. Reisman		
_____	Trade paper__ __ __ __	8.95	_____
_____	Hard cover __ __ __ __	16.95	_____
_____•To Grow By Storybook Readers—Janet Friend 44.95 per set		_____
	Shipping and Handling		_____
	TOTAL		_____

•New Titles

AVAILABLE AT BOOKSTORES EVERYWHERE or order direct from:
Huntington House Publishers • P.O. Box 53788 • Lafayette, LA 70505

Send check/money order. For faster service use VISA/MASTERCARD, call
toll-free 1-800-749-4009
Add: Freight and handling, $2.00 for the first book ordered, and $.50 for each
additional book.

Enclosed is $ ——————— including postage.
Card type:
VISA/MASTERCARD# ————————————————— Exp. Date _____
Name ——————————————————————————————
Address ————————————————————————————
City, State, Zipcode ——————————————————————